D1028706

# THE PURSUIT

*Success*
*is*
*hidden*
*in*
*the*
*journey.*

## by Dexter Yager and John Mason
with Steve Yager

# More Praise for The Pursuit

> "Dexter Yager will make you feel the intimate connection between success and failure. He'll help you understand how to harness failure to make it pull you to success. Here's a sharp, thoughtful, quirky, and ultimately potent piece of how-to literature. The pursuit and attainment of real freedom is the meaning of life. Buy *The Pursuit*. Read. Re-read. Then go do it."

**— Jamie Clarke**, *Mount Everest Climber and Author of* The Power of Passion

> "This book, *The Pursuit*, is a masterpiece. It's simple yet profound, common sense but not common practice. This book will empower you to live a full life and to die empty. It will create in you a hunger for a better life. Dexter is the message that he brings, his life example is that it's possible and necessary that we never stop dreaming. Dexter, I'm proud of you. This is your brother from another mother."

**— Les Brown**, *Author of* Live Your Dreams, It's Not Over Until You Win

> "I have enormously enjoyed the times that I have spent with Dexter Yager because his philosophy and my philosophy for success in life are so similar. Even though I am a pediatric neurosurgeon and he is more of a businessman, the mindset that creates success is still the same. I was very excited when I recognized how helpful this would be to individuals who are attempting to take control of their lives and to improve their environment."

**— Benjamin S. Carson, Sr., M.D.**, *Author of* Gifted Hands, *Professor of Neurological Surgery, Oncology, Plastic Surgery, and Pediatrics Johns Hopkins Medical Institutions*

> "There is a wealth of material in this book to help you become successful in every area of life. Dexter has a unique ability to take common sense logic and apply it to every day life in a way that makes winners out of losers. *The Pursuit* is all about dreaming the dream, living the victory and winning at life. This is one of the best books I have ever read."

**— Dr. Jerry Falwell**, *Founder and Chancellor Liberty University, Lynchburg, Virginia*

> "*The Pursuit* is a remarkable collection of wisdom from an extraordinary man. Dexter is an inspirational teacher whose insightful understanding of how to become successful has reached thousands of people. This book is a must-read for any one that has a dream and a goal."

**— Alex Spanos** , *Real Estate Investor, Entrepreneur, Owner of the San Diego Chargers, Author of* Sharing The Wealth

> "When the wise talk, the wise listen. Dexter Yager sculptures Life-Champions. I have read his books, scrutinized his endurance and followed his instructions. His reactions prove his greatness. His decisive responses to Adversity, Pain, Problems, and Success easily explain why millions are transformed and unleashed through his mentorship. Dexter is simply...The Master Mentor. His remarkable love for people has removed a million heartaches...and unlocked the secret of Greatness in every one of us who have received the Golden Gift of Access to him. His newest book, *The Pursuit*, is an irreplaceable Gold Mine."

— **Dr. Mike Murdock**, *Pastor & Author of the* Wisdom Commentary Collection *of books*


> "Dexter Yager has dedicated his life to helping others. His pursuit is to motivate people to achieve their dreams."

— **Sue Myrick**, *U.S. Congresswoman*


> "A great book for showing the freedom and joy in owning your own business. Plus, the authors give you the secret of making your business last!"

— **Dr. Gary Smalley**, *One of the country's best known authors and speaker on family relationships*


> "Dexter Yager is a great American, a great mentor and a great guy. He will help you, motivate you, and inspire you to get excited about your dreams and go for them."

— **Dave Thomas**, *Late founder of Wendy's*


> "Have you ever realized how unique you are and how God has positioned you for success? If not, you will want to read the treasury of knowledge and classic wisdom embedded in this book. It is literally the journey of a dream come true, and the appreciation of the journey to get there."

— **Dr. Charles Stanley**, *Senior Pastor, First Baptist Church Atlanta, President of In Touch Ministries*


> "As an immigrant who came to the United States in search of the American dream, I have found no one who epitomizes the spirit of free enterprise more than Dexter Yager. His resilient style and practical no-nonsense approach has taken many to uncharted heights. His advice and insight will allow you to unleash the success hidden within you as you pursue your own journey."

— **Krish Dhanam**, *Vice President of Zig Ziglar Corporation, Speaker & Author of* The American Dream from an Indian Heart


> "This book proves that we all have greater inner dreams, and those dreams are only able to come into fruition when we follow the pursuit of determination, and the inner faith that within each of us lies as dormant-miracles just waiting to be born."

— **Marva Collins**, *Pioneered a methodology of teaching failed and uneducatable-labeled children, through a curriculum of tough love and discipline, with moral values and self worth, to become academic scholars.*

# Dedication

This book is dedicated to everyone who is currently pursuing a worthwhile dream, no matter what that dream may be. The success may be found in the destination, but the true rewards lie in the journey.

Henry Ford says, "I do not believe that a man can ever leave his business. He ought to think of it by day and dream of it by night." I agree. I believe that anyone can fall in love with success, but it takes a real winner to fall in love with the work required to become successful. Success is a habit, something you do daily, and you get there one step at a time.

Whether you're just beginning your journey or are many years down the road, I want you to remember one thing: you've got what it takes. Now take what you've got and go do it. If you can see it, you can be it!

**You gotta believe,**
Dexter Yager

*All of Dexter's proceeds from this book are being donated to the* **Yager Freedom Foundation**—*a foundation dedicated to preserving and perpetuating the Judeo-Christian principles that our nation was founded upon.*

# Contents

# Introduction

Are you stumbling toward an uncertain future? Or, are you ready to wholeheartedly pursue your dream? There are million dollar ideas around you every day...do you see them? You can see a thousand miracles every day, or you can see nothing. Your big opportunity is right where you are now. As Earl Nightingale said, "You are, at this moment, standing right in the middle of your own 'acres of diamonds'."

There is a master key that unlocks life's possibilities. Dreams are good, but not good enough. Faith is good, but not good enough. Goals are good, but not good enough. There's only one way to prove your faith, dreams and goals...only one way to transform them into a reality. The pursuit.

The most important thing you can ever do in life is find a dream worth chasing—and when you catch it, find a bigger one. Pursuit changes everything. It captivates your heart, increases your momentum, unleashes focus and brings astonishing results.

You will find that happiness is chasing your dreams, not only in reaching them. A major corporate study of sixty-two business leaders all over the world, from Marriott Corporation to Apple Computer, revealed that not one of the leaders was a classic workaholic as we picture them: grim, driven, enslaved by work but compelled to do it anyway. Instead, they were actually "workaphiles," lovers of work. They absolutely loved doing what they did! The right pursuit brought joy and success.

Dr. Charles Garfield added, "Peak performers are people who are committed to a compelling mission. It is very clear that they care deeply about what they do and their efforts, energies, and enthusiasms are traceable back to that particular mission." Proverbs 19:21 says, "Whatever your plan is, just know that nothing else will satisfy you." You're not truly free until you actively pursue and have been made captive by your supreme mission in life.

Unfortunately, the average person's life consists of 20 years of having parents ask where he or she is going, 40 years of having a spouse ask the same question, and at the end, the mourners wondering the same. Martin Luther King Jr. said, "If a man hasn't discovered something that he will die for, he isn't fit to live."

Success always starts with a dream that seems impossible, but when that dream is pursued and worked, over time it gradually comes true. Nothing worthwhile happens overnight. The road to success runs uphill; so don't expect to break any speed records. Success takes time. Once you get your dream going, you have to maintain its momentum. You can't afford to stop along the way. The hardest thing to do in pursuing your dream is to get it rolling from a standing stop. You want to have to do that only once—the first time.

The world makes room for a person on a pursuit. Like a fire truck with its lights on or a police car with its sirens blaring, people may not know where you're going but they know you're off to something important. For the tenacious there is always time and opportunity. Don't be caught out in the backyard looking for four-leaf clovers when opportunity knocks at your front door.

Every morning in Africa a gazelle wakes up. It knows that it must outrun the fastest lion, or it will be eaten. Every morning in Africa a lion wakes up. It knows that it must outrun the slowest gazelle, or it will starve to death. It doesn't matter whether you're a lion or a gazelle; when the sun comes up you'd better be running.

In your heart there is a sleeping lion roaring from the inside out, intently desiring a pursuit worthy of placement by God above. Choose to be on a mission. "When you discover your mission, you will feel its demand. It will fill you with enthusiasm and a burning desire to get to work on it." (W. Clement Stone). Successful lives are motivated by dynamic pursuit.

A lazy man is judged by what he doesn't pursue. Albert Hubert remarked, "Parties who want milk should not seat themselves on a stool in the middle of the field and hope that the cow will back up to them." The choice of stopping or pursuing is a defining moment in your life.

When a person makes a decision to pursue, the facts don't count. The past doesn't count. The odds don't count.

I don't know about you, but dandelions pursue me. Everywhere I've lived, at every house I've owned, they've followed me. But I've learned something very important from that pesky little plant. Our daily prayer should be, "Lord, give me the determination and tenacity of a weed."

Dig for diamonds, don't chase butterflies. Life is too short to think small. Pursue and march off the map. Go where you have never gone before.

Nothing brings greater joy to the heart of a leader, parent, or spouse than to see a man or a woman pursuing their purpose in life. Now is the time to climb out of the grandstands and onto the playing field!

It's said that a person's future can be determined by their

daily habits. The Pursuit contains 31 chapters—a month's worth of proven success principles. It takes roughly 10-15 minutes to read one chapter per day. By reading just one chapter a day, you'll be developing an essential success habit that will stay with you long after you've finished this book.

*The Pursuit* is a short and quick, yet extremely powerful read. The more times you read it, the better you'll understand the wisdom and be able to incorporate it into your own life. Also, *The Pursuit* was written in a conversational style that makes it easy to pull out important points. Underline the passages that effect you the most. When you've finished the book, go back and re-read your underlines over and over.

When you finish the book, be sure to apply the information immediately. Immediate action will help you understand and remember the information. Applied knowledge equals results.

May this book move you further along in the journey toward your dreams.

Welcome to the pursuit.

# Chapter 1

## The number one thing that controls us

*It is not so much a tragedy to be a person with no eyesight,
but it is a great tragedy to have no vision.*
**- Helen Keller**

Each of us has the potential and opportunity for success. It takes just as much effort to lead an unproductive life as it does an effective life, and it always costs more not to do what's right than to do what is right. Still, millions lead aimless lives in prisons of their own making—simply because they haven't decided what to do with their lives.

> **It's not the absence of things that makes you unhappy, but the absence of vision.**

"A lot of people confuse bad decision-making with destiny" (Kin Hubbard). "Where there is no vision the people perish," says the book of Proverbs. It's not the absence of things that makes you unhappy, but the absence of vision.

A leader's job is to look into the future and see the organization...not as it is, but as it can be. If you are not spending more time in the future (thinking and planning) than in the past and present, you are likely to continue living the life you are living today.

> **The impact of any person is determined by the cause for which they live and the price they are willing to pay.**

You can predict a person's future by their awareness of their destiny. Life's heaviest burden is to have nothing to carry. The impact of any person is determined by the cause for which they live and the price they are willing to pay.

If there's anything Americans need now, more than ever, it's more dreams, more vision. Your vision controls your future. People that cannot see it cannot do it. But once you start to see it, you start to see something that you want more. It's the next step of your vision. But you need a vehicle to get there.

The impossible becomes possible when you get the picture right. All my successes in life started happening when I got the picture right.

How did Birdie and I get to where we are? We had a vision of where we wanted to be. We read books. We created mentors out of our books because we had nobody to look to, nobody that was counseling us, nobody that was helping us, nobody that had the success we wanted, and so I had to put together my plan and I depended upon the power of prayer. God is ultimately in control.

**Vision marks the path to victory so that everyone can move in the same direction together.**

A lot of people no longer hope for the best; they just hope to avoid the worst. Too many have heard opportunity knocking at their door, but by the time they unhooked the chain, pushed back the bolt, turned two locks and shut off the burglar alarm—it was gone!

People generally have too many opinions and not enough convictions. A person going nowhere can be sure of reaching his destination.

A vision is like a treasure map with "X marks the spot." Vision marks the path to victory so that everyone can move in the same direction together. Are you going to mark your victory? Are you going to decide where you are going?

There had to be a first Kennedy. There had to be a first Rockefeller and there has to be a first rich guy with your name. Is it going to be you, or is it going to be one of the next generations? Are you going to change your financial position for your family? You can do it, with vision.

**People generally have too many opinions and not enough convictions.**

Your vision must be bigger than you. Learn to be comfortable with great dreams. Unless you take on more than you can possibly do, you will never do all that you can. Don't listen to those who say, "It's not done that way." Don't listen to those who say, "You're taking too big a chance." Develop an infinite capacity to ignore what others say can't be done.

Boldness in vision is the first, second and third most important thing. If you dare nothing you should expect nothing. What you need is an idea. Be brave enough to live creatively. "Since it doesn't cost a dime to dream, you'll never shortchange yourself when you stretch your imagination" (Robert Schuller). A single idea—the sudden flash of any thought—may be worth a million dollars. Look at things not as they are, but as they can be. Vision adds value to everything.

# Chapter 1

Use your imagination to create a clear vision (mental picture) of something you would like to see happen in your life—it may even be a feeling you want to feel. Continue to focus on that idea, picture, or feeling until you realize it. Crystallizing a vision of the future we want is creating the future in advance.

Man cannot discover new oceans unless he has the courage
to lose sight of the shore.
**- Andre Gide**

The best way to predict the future is to create it.
**- Stephen Covey**

Where there is no vision the people will perish.
**- Proverbs**

# Chapter 2

## Freedom—there's nothing like it

You cannot truly experience the freedom available in this or any other country
unless you have economic freedom.

**- Dexter Yager**

I was not number one in my class, and I didn't go to college. You know why? I knew where I was going before I went to college, so I didn't go. I knew what I wanted to be—I wanted to be in business for myself. And most of the guys teaching business courses aren't in business. I'd already learned the course by working for businessmen as a kid. If everything that you are depends upon a piece of paper that you've got, then you aren't anything.

John Foster said, "It is a poor disgraceful thing not to be able to reply, with some degree of certainty, to the simple questions, 'What will you be? What will you do?'" Dr. Charles Garfield said, "Peak performers are people who are committed to a compelling mission. It is very clear that they care deeply about what they do and their efforts, energies and enthusiasms are traceable back to that particular mission." You're not truly free until you've been made captive by your mission in life.

Teaching people how to get good jobs is not the answer. Why would your parents invest so much money to educate you to go out and get a job when you can have your own business? You could start into a lot of businesses for less money than the biggest and the most prestigious colleges charge students to attend one year.

A job...I had one once. Is this what a job means? I get up in the morning, go to work, get time off for lunch, go to work, come home, back and forth, back and forth. Get a 2-week vacation, go visit relatives and friends. That's a life? Gets to be a rut. What's the difference between a rut and a grave? Ruts have the ends knocked out. If you don't have a dream, you're in the grave already. At least I've got a "good" job. The only good job you can have is working for yourself when you own the company. People come and say, "Well I've got a good job." I don't know what a good job is. I don't know of a good job you cannot get fired from. I didn't want to come home someday and tell my wife and kids, "they got rid of me." I'd seen too many companies close.

> **One of the biggest mistakes you can make is to think that having a good job leads ultimately to wealth.**

I'd seen too many situations happen. I knew owning your own business was the only way it didn't matter; the freedom was worth the struggle. It was better to know what was going on because I was the owner, than wondering what was going on because I was an employee.

One of the biggest mistakes you can make is to think that having a good job leads ultimately to wealth. I asked a young telephone receptionist in Columbus, Ohio, to tell me her idea of the most important factor in wealth acquisition. She replied, "Having a good job, a great job." I was surprised by how often the same answer was given by those whose income is average and below. Millionaires rarely respond this way. It is commonly held in our society that finding a good job, working hard and moving up the ladder to more responsibility will eventually take us to golden retirement years of wealth and happiness. The fact of the matter is that a job merely supports the habits we have, like eating, but it rarely leads to wealth and never leads to freedom.

If you want freedom, dream big. Have faith in yourself. How big is your God? Dream Big!

**We weren't looking for big cars, big homes, swimming pools, and vacations. I was looking for freedom.**

One of the first goals I set was that my wife would never have to go to work again. My second goal was that I would never have to report to anybody or go to a job again. One of my third goals was to help all my friends have a great lifestyle.

When I got in business 40 years ago, Birdie and I had a dream. Our dream was to make two and a half times what I had been making in my job and HAVE FREEDOM! We weren't looking for big cars, big homes, swimming pools, and vacations. I was looking for freedom. I wanted to be in control of my life. I didn't want somebody making my decisions. We wanted the freedom to choose how much we wanted to work and when we wanted to work.

Now, there's something that's vital to understand. You're either committed or not. My first goal was I wanted to be free. I was not competing with anybody else in business, and there was a thing inside of me that screamed, "You aren't going to be a jerk and work for somebody else the rest of your life."

Don't say, "What would my friends think?" Do your friends rule you? Do they pay your bills? Do they make your decisions? That means you aren't in charge. I want to be in charge of my life. That means I make the decisions, not a jury of people making my decisions, approving what I do. Then I'm not free. I don't know who I am if they're making the decisions.

Today we live a good life, and we have freedom. We make a lot of money. How much money do we make? I don't know. When you know how much you make you don't make much. When you know how much you are worth you are not worth much...THAT'S FREEDOM! Freedom is not free. There is a price to pay. What would you be willing to do to experience real freedom? For me I hated to travel, I hated not to sleep in my own bed and to be away from my family. I knew the people who made the big money traveled. They expanded their territory. Looking back it was a small price to pay for a lifetime of expanded choices.

I remember going to a business meeting where it was advertised that Norman Vincent Peale was going to be speaking. It was the first time I'd ever gone to see him; I'd only read his books. I sat at a round table at the front because there were a couple of seats open. Nobody seemed to sit there, so I came up. I wanted to hear him real bad, I wanted to sit right in front of him, so I sat there with my tape recorder and I taped the whole talk. After the meeting was over, a man sitting next to me at the table said, "Mr. Yager." We introduced ourselves to each other. He asked what I did for a living, I said I was a marketing consultant, and he said, "I'd like to have your address." The next day he showed up at my house in a limousine with a chauffeur, wanted to buy the tape from me and, on top of that, he said, "I'd like you to come work for me." I said, "Uh, what would you like me to do? I've got my own business, I'm happy." He said, "I'd like you to train my sales people, your card says you're a marketing consultant; I'd like you to help my people with their market."

I sat down and I explained to him, "Look, I'm in a business and I use the term 'marketing consultant' as a general introduction to my potential parters. I don't have any marketing degrees or anything." He said, "How about $60,000 a year?," I said, "You don't seem to understand." He said, "You don't seem to understand. I want you. I own this large company called Pittsburgh Steel," and he went on and he's telling me all about it. He said, "I need a guy with guts, like you." I said, "Well I've got my own business." He said, "How about one day a week, $60,000 a year?" "No." "$90,000?" "No!"

> When you know how much you make you don't make much. When you know how much you are worth you are not worth much.

I was thinking all that time, "Wow, nobody's ever offered me this before and I have to say no because of my dream and he's upping the ante and throwing anything in and no matter what I tell him about myself, he wants me." I realized later, that I was a guy just like him. He wanted me; whatever time I gave would be worth a lot more than somebody would give him full-time. He wanted my dream and my commitment. But it was like a big bonus check to me just to know I could say, "NO! I DON'T NEED A JOB; YOU CAN'T OFFER ME ENOUGH MONEY!" I knew what freedom was worth.

Freedom is the Almighty God's gift to every man
and woman in this world.
- **President George W. Bush**

# Chapter 3

## Only where Free Enterprise exists

*My God! How little do my countrymen know what precious blessings they are in possession of, and which no other people on earth enjoy!*
**- Thomas Jefferson**

What the free enterprise system really means is that the more enterprising you are, the freer you are. What we all need is emphasis on free and even more on enterprise.

The majority of people do not understand free enterprise, and you've got to learn to accept free enterprise to be the leader. In America, we've got two kinds of wealth. We've got wealth that created itself, and those are normally guys that are conservatives. And then we've got a bunch of guys that are fourth-and fifth-generation wealth, and they're some of the biggest leaders in the Socialism movement. And they feel guilty about being rich because they don't understand that somebody else paid the price that they aren't having to pay.

> No matter how you slice it there are only two groups in America—the producers and the non-producers.

No matter how you slice it there are only two groups in America—the producers and the non-producers. But thank God for the "producers", because the hope of America and the world is the free enterprise system.

Right after Ronald Reagan got elected as president, a

couple of people came up to me and said, "Dexter, you worked so hard on Reagan's campaign. We owe you something. Would you consider the next ambassadorship that comes open?" That would mean moving to another country to be a very distinguished ambassador from America. I said, "I didn't do anything wrong. Why do I have to leave America? That's no reward." I believe in America. That's where my hope is.

Many people in America think somebody owes them a living. Instead, every American owes all the people that made America great. We don't appreciate what we have, so we don't utilize anywhere near our potential. We are a blessed nation, but when we are always blaming somebody else, we can't count our blessings.

If you study the history of World War II and you study America's role in it, what did we do? After we beat our enemies, we went in and helped them rebuild. We taught them the free enterprise system. We taught them the way we manufactured, the way we plan ahead. We taught them all the advantages. We're the only ones who came back and helped make it a better place. We had a choice of one of two things: to whip them and walk away, have them hate us and try to build up and retaliate, or go in and teach them how we have the freedoms and lifestyle we have. America has the greatest lifestyle of any country in the world.

**Never in history have we needed a new commitment to the free enterprise system more than we do right now.**

You see, only in America could the men and women

who have the largest dreams, investments, and work the hardest, believe they should be rich. God made the rules. God's a free enterpriser. The only countries that have gone and continued to grow are the free enterprise countries.

We work to create morals and levels of achievement for ourselves to prove we're somebody. When we take and create all kinds of equality, we've taken away all the incentives in life, and then we'll all become nobodies. Everybody will be a nobody. When we fight for equality, we cannot ever achieve it because God did not make it. All we'll do is create destruction. When you give a man a position because of equality you take away the rights of the guy in the identical race, religion, or whatever that he has achieved on his own. I believe you give poor people an opportunity, not a handout.

**God's a free enterpriser.**

It's normally the poor kids that get tired of being poor who grow up without anything going for them that say, "I'm going to change it. I'm not going to have to live this way all of my life. I will start a business. I will make it big. I will succeed." The new rich normally come from poverty. And the ones that never get rich are the ones that Mom and Dad did everything for them and never made them pay the price for performance on their own. That's why you build your free enterprise system. It's why you build your wealth. That's why you have your lifestyle. You're building your own dream so someday when the boss says, "I don't like you doing that thing," you can say, "Bye-bye. I don't need your job."

Every time you get something for nothing, you make

somebody more of a nothing than a something. You understand that? Every time you take from the rich to give to the poor, you keep the poor poorer. You take incentive away to be rich. The more you give them to survive, the less reason they have to work. It doesn't matter whether you're government or whether you're a parent.

Free enterprise is all about trying to raise everybody as high as you can get them. But the first thing you've got to do is raise their thinking and raise their dream and know that they've got to propel themselves. And for a lot of us that's hard.

Only in America could a guy who stuttered, who barely graduated from high school, ever dream of being asked to be a speaker in front of thousands and meet with Presidents. See, it's only in America that a

**Commitment to work or commitment to leisure brings different results.**

24-year-old father can invest less than a hundred dollars to start his own business and be able to earn and learn. Commitment to work or commitment to leisure brings different results. Never in history have we needed a new commitment to the free enterprise system more than we do right now.

Rich DeVos used to always tell the story about the young kid they were so worried about because the kid got to be one year old, two years old, three years old, four years old, five years old, who never uttered a word, never a "mama, papa," no nothing. At six years old, Mom served breakfast.

The kid took his hot chocolate, and said, "Oh! That's terrible!" The parents stood there astounded. "Oh my! First words and it's a sentence!—If you could talk, how come it took you this long?" "Everything's been okay up 'til now." The people who deserve a better lifestyle are the ones that work. See?

You know what the best way is to teach somebody how to solve their problems? It is solving your own problems. The more problems you have, the more you will solve. The more experience you have gotten the easier it is to help somebody else through their problems. Reaching in your pocket and saying "Well, friends, here is some money; this will solve your problems" is never the answer. The answer is, "I have got some dollars that I have earned to help me solve my problems. Now, let me show you how to make some dollars to help you solve your problems."

My job is to get you the knowledge, so you can think on your own, make your own decisions. And to be candid with you, I've been rich, and I've been poor. I like rich best. And you know what? I want everybody in America to have the opportunity to get rich. It's in getting rich that you help the economy. When you get rich, you may need somebody to go out and do some shopping for you. People to do this, and people to do that. The more successful people get, the more people they hire to do other things they used to do themselves. So, the real goal in America should be that we would have more people getting richer than ever before in the history of America because they would be hiring more people. The more money I make, the better I can live, the better lifestyle my kids get used to, the better they'll want to work, and harder they'll want to commit themselves to have a better future than Mom and Dad because most kids try to do better than Mom and Dad. The hope of the world is a free enterprise system.

Free enterprise is an enterprise free of government interference. Capitalism is an economic system characterized by private or corporate ownership of goods, and by prices, production, and the distribution of goods that are determined mainly by competition in a free market.
**- Bob McEwen**

Free enterprise isn't a gift. We have to work to maintain it. The only political or economic system in which we have no risk is one in which we also have no choice. If we forget that, we lose everything.
**- Rich DeVos**

# Chapter 4

## Who are you?

This above all: to thine own self be true.
- **William Shakespeare**

Driving down the road yesterday I saw a bumper sticker that made me honk at the driver and give him a big "thumbs up." It said, "I would rather be hated for what I am than loved for what I am not." You've got to know who you really are. When you know who you are you don't have to prove who you are to everybody else.

For example, some guys went out to meet this guy. And going down through the airport a couple of kids tried to throw a punch at him. Half fun, but 90 percent real. And they thought "Boy I'd like to knock him out." The guy they were messing with was Muhammad Ali. He didn't try to prove something by punching back (and knocking them all out). Instead he just said, "Hi." He knows who he is.

A middle aged woman had a heart attack and was taken to the hospital. While on the operating table she had a near-death experience. Seeing God, she asked if this was it. God said, "No you have another 43 years, 2 months, and 8 days to live.

Upon recovery the woman decided to stay in the hospital and have a face lift, liposuction, tummy tuck, etc. She even had someone come in and change her hair color, figuring since she had so much more time to live, she might as well make the most of it. She got out of the hospital after the last operation and while crossing the street she was killed by an ambulance speeding to the hospital.

Arriving in front of God, she demanded, "I thought you said I had another forty years?"

God replied, "I didn't recognize you."

Be yourself. Think about it: Aren't most of the discontented people you know trying to be something they are not, or trying to do something they're not supposed to do? "The reward for conformity was that everyone liked you except yourself." (Rita Mae Brown)

> **Everybody who ever became great was a nobody who one day decided to be a somebody.**

Everybody who ever became great was a nobody who one day decided to be a somebody. They were all nobodies who decided to be somebodies. I'm just wondering when are you going to decide to be somebody? How about now?

Your potential is whatever you make it. One of the hardest things about climbing the ladder of success is getting through the crowd of copies at the bottom. The number of people who don't take advantage of their talents is more than made up for by the number who take advantage of the talents they scarcely have. You are a specialist. You are not created to be all things to all people. You are the greatest miracle in the world. Stand out, don't blend in!

When we look down on ourselves, we look down on our God. He didn't make a mistake when he made you.

Don't let anybody ever tell you that. None of us are perfect, and if we were, nobody would recognize it because a lot of people are out to criticize anybody anyway. When they pick on us they feel better about themselves. So let's let them feel better about themselves. Let's not take it personally. When they pick on us it's a sign of a poor self image on their part. Let's recognize it, let's get going and let's get ourselves into what's good.

You and I don't want to be equal, isn't that right? And you can never make the loser a winner until he decides to change. What you don't use you lose, and I have created a lot of bad habits in my life that I had to change. I used to have a terrible habit. Every time I did something that was wrong, I said "Why you idiot. Stupid Dexter, why did you do that?" I had to learn to quit calling myself stupid idiot. How many ever do something like that, call yourself stupid idiot? Never do it again. You're not stupid, you're not an idiot, and quit putting yourself down. And don't let your friends, the politicians or anybody else put you into a category that you don't want to live in.

> The biggest enemy most of us will face is ourselves. That nagging voice that says, "Be like him, you're not worthy, do what she does, go where the crowd is going."

You were made on purpose for a purpose. There is something for you to do that no one else can do as well as you can. Out of billions of applicants, you're the most qualified.

It's been said that the biggest enemy of great is good.

The biggest enemy most of us will face is ourselves. That nagging voice that says, "Be like him, you're not worthy, do what she does, go where the crowd is going." When you are trying to be like someone else, the best you can ever be is second best.

Let me tell you, in every generation there's going to be a certain amount of people that are going to take over all the industries. Everybody will say, "Well, it's too late for that." It's not too late for anything. The biggest churches have not been built yet. The biggest businesses have not been built yet. You are a champion hiding in a shell. When are you going to break through your shell and find out who's in there? If you're going to change anybody's way of thinking, first, you've got to change your way of thinking about you. Don't find yourself saying what the great evangelist Dwight L. Moody said: "I've never met a man who gave me as much trouble as myself."

You must begin to think of yourself as becoming the person you want to be. "Give the man you'd like to be a look at the man you are" (Edgar Guest). Change what you tell yourself. "No one really knows enough to be a pessimist" (Norman Cousins). Remember, "One of the nice things about problems is that a good many of them do not exist except in our imaginations" (Steve Allen). The fear you fear is only in yourself and nowhere else. There are two forces warring against each other inside us. One says, "You cannot!" and the other says, "With God, you can!"

How do you picture yourself? I was reading a newspaper column by a friend of mine, Jeffrey Gitomer, in which he referenced a book I read years ago. The book was *Psycho-Cybernetics* by Dr. Maxwell Maltz. In it, Maltz says, "We react to the image we have of ourselves in our brain. Change that image for the better, and our lives improve. Self-image is changed for the better or worse, not by intellect alone, not by intellectual knowledge alone, but by experiencing."

This applies to any aspect of your life, whether it's finding business success or anything else. You have to be able to picture yourself doing something first, before you can actually do it.

No one is in control of your destiny but you. You not only control your mind, but you also have the power to change the environment you're in. That's why I always say, "no excuses!" If you don't like where you're at, change it! If you change your self-image,

> **If you want the good stuff, find out who's got the good stuff. Make them your mentors.**

you will begin to change your mental image as well, and eventually your thoughts will become reality.

You know, if you put a hundred men side by side at the age of twenty-five, by the time they're sixty-five only one will be rich. Everything seemed equal. Why do some out-distance others? It's the way they think, who they pick as mentors, who they follow and how they view themselves. If ninety percent of the people you talk to about your dream laugh at you and then you want them to accept you, you can say goodbye to your dream. It's lost, lost by choice. If you want the good stuff, find out who's got the good stuff. Make them your mentors. People who have big dreams think differently than other people. The reason why some people are rich and others are poor is the way they think and the way they follow through.

I'm prejudiced about everybody. Everybody's special in some way. Sometimes Birdie and I are introduced as a royal couple. I am royalty. My middle name is Royal. How would you like to have Royal as your middle name? I got kidded a lot when I was a kid. Dexter Maltose. I got picked on for this weird name my parents gave me. But my Mom told me Dexter was her maiden name. She made me proud of the name Dexter. My grandfather, my dad's dad was Royal Jay Yager. I got his name. I got her name. I got the family name. I'm prejudiced. I'm proud of it. Get prejudiced about you. Be proud of who you are.

> **People would worry less about what others think about them if they only realized how seldom they do.**

Be proud of where you came from. Be proud of your kids. Too many people predict to the kids that they are going to be losers. Identify their winner traits. Okay? Find what's right with them and edify what's right.

What are you going to be? Who are you going to be? What are you going to do? God created you and He doesn't create any junk. I don't care if you're purple with black and white spots all over you. God only made one of you; be proud of that. I'm 5' 6", that's what I've got to work with. I wanted to be 6' 5." Somehow the numbers got flip-flopped.

But I found out, it's not how tall you are outside, it's how tall you are inside. Now, we're all different. God didn't make two of us. He made one of you and there's good and bad in you. Which do you want to focus on?

A lot of people in America are taking stands for what they're not. They end up spending their whole lives as strangers to themselves. When Birdie and I knew where we came from and what we thought of ourselves, we didn't think we were anybody special, or that we could ever be anybody special, but then we've seen ourselves step out and make decision after decision. And when you get out there, and you learn how, step by step, by trial and error, by falling and getting back up, and you get good and you start passing the rest, then you start realizing anybody can do this. Then you find out the major American disease is not AIDS. The major disease in America is a poor self-image—people that don't think they've got what it takes. You've got to take what you've got and develop it. And then, all of a sudden, you go like, "Me? Do that? Ok, I'll try. Well, I'll try again. Oh my! Look what I've done." You'll blow your own mind.

But when you don't know who you are, you can get hung up and screwed up over any little thing. You know what I mean? So that's why I just love to see people who can learn to be who they are early on in their life, learn to be real, learn to have fun, and not worry all the time about what everybody else is thinking about them. People would worry less about what others think about them if they only realized how seldom they do. They're not worrying about you; they're wondering about what you're thinking about them!

It's amazing along the way as you go toward success, whether you're a young kid, or whether you're forty or fifty, someone is always going to be deciding what your spot in life is. How valuable you are. How you should think and how you should be. But in life you've got to make the final decision about you because it's your life. The old saying is true, "If you don't decide what's important in your life, someone else will decide for you."

You know it's awful important to know who you are. Most people don't know who they are, and they let everybody else around them tell them who they are. I'm here to tell you that what your friends have told you is wrong. You are a winner but only by choice. I'm a winner by choice. It wasn't an accident; it was a decision. A successful self-image is just a decision away.

What are you going to be today? Are you letting the world control you and keep you from being successful? Not me, not me. This valuable decision forces you to do what you've got to do. You've got to learn how to make you produce because, see, you're the greatest asset you'll ever have.

Nobody else is going to respect you before you start to respect yourself. The problem is when you look at yourself and you look for a defect, or you hide behind a defect versus developing a pride and going after a dream regardless of the facts, because every winner has to overcome something. Your power is in your personal belief.

Achievement is life. It is what it is all about. The chance to get rid of this lousy self-image that the schools and the wise guys seem to cram down everybody's throat. Many of our parents, loved ones, teachers, sisters, brothers, cousins, preachers, congressmen, senators, the media and everybody around treats us and teaches us that we are less than the best, and it's wrong. Ninety percent of everything we have been taught all our lives is wrong. And until you and I wake up to it and realize that they're wrong, you're not going to move. You've got to realize that God made you and me, and God doesn't make junk. He makes the best.

Dare to be who you are.

Knowing others is intelligence; knowing yourself is true wisdom. Mastering others is strength; mastering yourself is true power.
**– Lao Tzu**

Success begins by raising the opinion we have of ourselves.
**– Dexter Yager**

# Chapter 5

## The past is past

*Yesterday is history, tomorrow is a mystery, today is a gift from God, which is why we call it the present.*
**- Bill Keane**

Close the door on your past. "The past should be a springboard, not a hammock," said Edmund Burke. You can never plan the future by the past. Have you ever noticed that those to whom yesterday still looks big, aren't doing much today? Quit getting hung up on your past accomplishments or failures. Some of you are so hung up on your past or present that you're not seeing your future.

It is important to look forward. Your prosperity and destiny are there. In Philippians 3:13,14 (NIV), Paul said, "Forgetting what is behind and straining toward what is ahead, I press on toward the goal to win the prize for which God has called me heavenward in Christ Jesus." You can't walk backward into the future.

I like to listen to people. I specifically like to listen to the percent of time they spend talking about the past, present and future. I have found that those who predominately talk about the past are usually going backwards. Those that talk about the present are typically maintaining. But those who are talking about the future are growing.

Some people stay so far in the past that the future is gone before they get there. The future frightens only those who prefer living in the past. Living in the past is such an appalling waste of energy. You can't build on it. No one has ever backed into prosperity. You cannot have a better tomorrow if you are thinking about yesterday all day today.

The world is in your hands. Close your fingers, tighten your grasp; don't open your hands and let things slide through your fingers. Today is the first day of the rest of your life; all you've got is the future. The past is over. It doesn't matter what you've done or I've done, it's over. The door is closed; we can't change the past. From now on tomorrow is what counts—step out on faith. Come let God show you He's willing to work in your life. He wants you to succeed. He wants you to start living on faith, but it's in your hands. You can reject Him, you can reject me, you can reject this, but it doesn't mean you're right. You have the right to be wrong. It's your choice, and it's your future. You know the thing you've got to realize is that what you've got in your hands is the kind of information people need—you know, the kind that makes the difference.

> **Living in the past is such an appalling waste of energy. You can't build on it. No one has ever backed into prosperity.**

Don't rely on the past. You leave your past behind with a new dream. See, that's all it takes. It's going to take a lot of work, but you've got to start some place. You can't allow the do-nothings to tell you what your future is.

I agree with Laura Palmer's advice: "Don't waste today

regretting yesterday instead of making a memory for tomorrow." David McNally said, "Your past cannot be changed, but you can change your tomorrow by your actions today." Never let yesterday use up too much of today. It's true what Satchel Paige said, "Don't look back. Something may be gaining on you."

"Living in the past is a dull and lonely business; looking back strains the neck muscles, causing you to bump into people not going your way (Edna Ferber). The first rule for happiness is: avoid lengthy thinking on the past. Nothing is as far away as one hour ago." Charles Kettering added, "You can't have a better tomorrow if you are thinking about yesterday all the time." Your past doesn't equal your future.

It is one thing to learn about the past; it is another to wallow in it.
**- Kenneth Auchincloss**

# Chapter 6

## To have a dream come true you'll first need a dream

*If you believe it is worth it, you will be willing to look like a fool while you pursue your dream.*
**- The Wright brothers**

I really believe that the best way to live your life is "outside of the box." The future belongs to those who can think unthinkable thoughts, see where no one is looking and take action before it's obvious.

I used to have a habit when I lived in Rome, New York. There were two dream homes, one was my wife's dream home and the other one was mine. And I was willing to take either. It was a move ahead. But I used to go after every meeting and sit at least five minutes in front of each home. At least five minutes I'd just stare at it. I was moving that home into my subconscious mind. Then I would go down to the Cadillac garage. Every night, after every meeting, I'd look at every new Cadillac they had like I'd never seen them before. And I was putting that into my subconscious mind. I was courting those homes, courting those cars. Just like I courted my girlfriends. Putting them back there, where it was not a matter of, "it's a nice thing if we could ever have it." Instead it was like, "I've got to have these." I was taking them from a wish, to a want, to a need, to a got. When you start needing something, you're going to get it pretty soon.

When you really need it bad enough. See, the problem with a lot of people is they don't go out and haunt themselves and hurt real bad for something that they should really go for. You know? You've got to hurt for it.

One of the best things I can do is take you into a realm you cannot afford, let you look at it, touch it, and then take you away. You know as long as most people are hurting, they're growing. When they stop hurting, they stop having goals, and they stop growing. They've lost purpose. Can you see that happening?

The only objections that you really need to overcome are your own. Where are you going from here? Some of you will be tempted to stay where you are. Some of you are going to the top. And if you cannot believe it, you cannot do it. It doesn't matter what the odds are or what the potential is. Your confession becomes your possession.

> One of the best things I can do is take you into a realm you cannot afford, let you look at it, touch it, and then take you away.

My first step was learning to believe in me and to get a dream. My next step was to get another dream. Then I found out the biggest thing I had to do in my life is work hard enough on my dream because my dream was a tool. It was the thing that gave me the energy to perform at a level I didn't know I was capable of. People eliminate their own potential. My prayer for you today is, "God, touch each one of you with a dream that would never quit, with the confidence that you could do it, with holding power that you would stay in until you started to see it come true." And then He'd give you more holding power until you could see it become a reality.

How big is your dream? Leaders are dreamers. My biggest job is to try to get you to dream bigger. So you tell me where you want to be, and I can help you get there. I want you to go out and look at nicer homes, and I want you to look at them so much that you say, "I deserve one." And you go do the work to get it.

> I found out the biggest thing I had to do in my life is work hard enough on my dream because my dream was a tool. It was the thing that gave me the energy to perform at a level I didn't know I was capable of.

Then other people will want what you've got and they'll do whatever it takes to get it, right? You've got to get a dream. You've got to get something that you want so bad that you're willing to do whatever it takes. It's different for everybody. Find what you want badly enough and then find out how to go for it.

Goal setting is when you want to grow your faith. When I start moving with faith, what I do is write my goals down and I make a copy of them, and I get all my kids and Birdie to write their goals down, and I make a copy of them. I put the copy away in a special spot to be looked at one year from the time we wrote them. Then all of us get together and we pray over the goals and ask God to bless them and help us get them and sometimes I write forty-eight, fifty, thirty-eight or fifteen goals. I write all kinds of goals. I want a better relationship with God. I want a better relationship with my team, I want a better relationship with my kids. I want a new home, I want a new car, and you put down what kind of home and what kind of car. You've got to define what you want and you write those goals.

I believe that you have to have a reason. And you're never going to go too far if money is your only reason. My "reason" is save America and spread the hope. That's what my life is committed to. And I know I'm going to bring a lot of marriages together. I know that I'm going to do a lot of other things because I've got a "reason."

> **It's not the size of your income or the size of your town that is the difference; it's the size of your thinking.**

I would rather be with people that are doing something and going some place. It's not the size of your income or the size of your town that is the difference; it's the size of your thinking. It's the size of your dream, your commitment, and your desire. People go from a wish to a want to a need to a got. There are a lot of wishers around. I wish I had this. I wish I had that, and they just become wishy-washy people. You know, what we're really looking for is the guy that moves out of that wishing area to wanting. I want that. Then it moves to I need it. I've got to have it. I've got it.

That's why until you move from "I wish" and "I try" and

"I hope" to "I will" and "I need" and "I'm going to", you're not going to get what you want; you cannot have it until you move. You've got to move from a weak position to a strong position. You've got to move from a wish to desire, and it turns you on fire.

We've had jets just because we started a little business with a little dream to make a thousand a month. And then I saw I could do more, I stretched, I pulled that brain a little bit, and I went dreaming. My net worth went up. My income went up. My comfort zone went up. The point is that I started dreaming.

When your dream stops progressing and you get comfortable, then you stop dreaming and you stop growing. People don't stop dreaming when they get old—people get old when they stop dreaming. So work on your dream. My number one dream is the number two person in my life. Birdie is my number two person. The number one person is my Lord and Savior.

> **People don't stop dreaming when they get old—people get old when they stop dreaming.**

While back in Rome, New York, we were with a couple of my high school buddies. I went and saw one of the guys I worked with who was my former boss at Sears, and he had just retired. He looks good. He's in good health. I asked him about his retirement program. Sears has a fabulous program. He told me what he got after working there forty-three years. It'd be a bad month for me. It's interesting. He's doing very well. He's got enough to retire and live well, but his whole retirement would not take care of the maintenance for one of my homes for a year. He was sharper than me. He was my boss. I was a young kid. What happened? Was I lucky or did I see a chance to pursue my own business, to have dreams, set goals, follow freedom? Where are you going to be five, ten, twenty or even one year from now?

Let your faith run ahead of your mind. See further than you can go and go further than you can see. Significant achievements have never been obtained by taking small risks on unimportant issues. "If you're hunting rabbits in tiger country, you must keep your eye peeled for tigers, but when you are hunting tigers you can ignore the rabbits" (Henry Stern). Don't be distracted by the rabbits. Set your sights on "big game." If you want a productive life you better have a dream that's big. It's got to be something you can barely obtain. When you set your goals high enough, that's how you become a champion some day.

---

### See further than you can go and go further than you can see.

---

The tragedy of life doesn't lie in not reaching your goals. The tragedy lies in not having any goals to reach.
**- Dr. Benjamin Mays**

# Chapter 7

## Winners come out of losers' positions

All of the significant battles are waged within the self.
**- Sheldon Kopp**

It's said that most of the superheros in the sports arena today came out of the poverty areas. What does that prove? Number one, it's not where you're at. It's not where you're from. It's not the race you're in. It proves the power of the dream.

> We don't succeed on our weaknesses. We succeed on our talent and our hunger.

People say, "You come from the wrong side of the tracks." Well which is the right side, left or right? I get tired of people that have been hanging on to the past for three, four, and five generations when they should be hanging on to the future.

I was from what I thought of as a big family. I was the second oldest of five kids. If you study birth order, the second kid normally doesn't make it. So how do you explain me? You break the mold when you get a dream.

We don't succeed on our weaknesses. We succeed on our talent and our hunger. If we're hungry enough for something, we change what we need to change, and we become what we need to become. We don't let the world run around and be prejudiced against us.

Don't restrict your thinking based on where you're from

or where you're at right now. I'll put it this way, "Don't live within your means." I'm not encouraging you to go wild, to have no boundaries, or to be reckless. Certainly we should spend within our means—but not live there. Talk with people smarter than you. Listen to those more spiritual than you. Ask questions of those more successful than you. Lend a hand to those less fortunate than you. Don't stay where you are.

If the shoe fits, don't wear it. If you do, you're not allowing room for growth. Webster knew all about the ineffectiveness of "living within your means." When you look up the word "means" in his dictionary, it tells you to see the word "average." When you decide to live within your means, you are deciding to live an average life.

I love it when somebody like Mugsy Bogues makes it. He was a professional basketball player who defied the odds. It's like he proved the facts don't count when the dream's big enough. I've always loved the guy that should never have been. Yet there he is, and he's a

**The most successful people have overcome the most.**

champion. And I'll never forget the news interview with two guys, one black, one white, that were like 6'5", 6'6" and got bumped off the team by Mugsy. I'd be embarrassed if I were 6'6" and a 5'3" guy knocked me off the basketball team. Wouldn't you? I've got the potential. It's no different than the story about David and Goliath. Even though he was just a little shepherd boy, David went after Goliath knowing he was a giant, and everybody was scared of him. But the reward was worth it, and the dream was worth it. What I heard a couple of times in the last year, is that David picked up five stones. Did you know that? He picked up five stones because he knew Goliath had four brothers. He was prepared to kill all five of them. Big dreamer. Again, the facts (5'3") don't count. In fact, the more you overcome, the more people respect you.

I get excited when I hear about what's right with America. I get excited when I hear what we're going to do—the changes that we can make. You and I are the ones that are going to change this country—change our home town, change our school system, change whatever you don't like. You and I have got to change it instead of complaining and griping about it. Don't you know that those who have come out of "losers' positions" know

> A lot of guys have got all kinds of potential, but they're afraid. They're afraid of what their friends are going to think.

better than anyone else what needs to be changed?

A lot of guys have got all kinds of potential, but they're afraid. They're afraid of what their friends are going to think. It's that stupid status. They get so involved in it that they don't realize that if you've got real friends, then they're going to like you no matter what you do. If they don't like you because of your dream, then they weren't really your friends.

I knew that stroke could not hold me down. The devil will try to steal your dream every possible way that he can. He'll hurt your relationship with people, with mates, with all things, but you cannot allow him to steal your dreams.

You've got to say, "I'm glued to the dream. I've got a purpose. You're not going to make junk out of me."

To come out of a loser's position, start with a dream. Our attitude makes a difference in our altitude in life. It absolutely affects how high you can go. It's up to us where we're going. It's not up to our boss, our father, or our mom. They give us guidance as far as they can, but it's up to us to make the necessary changes in life.

To launch past where you are, be different. Don't fit in with the majority. It keeps you going when everything would stop anybody else. The more you go through life, the more challenges there are. We are all special. We all have special talents. We all have special potential.

The most successful people have overcome the most. We cannot let our dreams go down the tube. We cannot talk about the problems; we've got to solve the problems. If you've got a problem, then find somebody that has the solution. Then you've got the answer, and you don't live on the problem. You live on the solution.

Adversity causes some men to break, others to break records.
- **William Arthur Ward**

The most expensive party you can throw is a pity party.
- **Dexter Yager**

One person with courage makes a majority.
- **Anonymous**

# Chapter 8

## Winners think alike

*What separates people most is not their background, their race, education or age, it's the way they think.*
**- Dexter Yager**

When I read books by people who have accumulated great wealth, I normally agree with almost everything they say. But it's amazing how many times I find losers who disagree with me and what these books say. But I understand why. Losers think differently than winners.

I've been through winning and losing. How many of you have had to reverse a lot of your thinking? I, too, have had to reverse a lot of my thinking on my journey from losing to winning. Every year I try to think better than I did the year before. Even today, we do things wrong. This shows others that we are not perfect or unique, and that we can achieve the things we have as well.

A lot of times people don't understand how much they have in them, and how we all need somebody to unlock the door to our hearts so that we can get rid of hang-ups. I love to see little kids; I always talk to them, tell them how cute they are, and how special they are. They haven't had the junk yet. They smile at you. I see some little girl and I sit there winking to see if I can get her to wink back. I mean it's special, isn't it? Sometimes some of the best winners to learn from are kids. We need to have an attitude like the youth do. Success is an attitude.

You can't be around winners and not get dividends. Winners think alike. If you want to be successful, then you've got to learn to be a good thinker, the right kind of thinker. There's the way that 10 percent see things, and then there's the way 90 percent see things. If you listen to the 90 percent, then you'll never be in the top 10 percent.

The greatest education outside of the word of God can be found in the story of those who have succeeded, what they've gone through, and what they've had to overcome.

**You've got to accept the fact that you have genius ability. Your mind is a muscle, and it's going to put out what you put in.**

Go listen to the people who are making it in the field you want. I had to go through the falling and the rebuilding of my business. And then I found *The Magic of Thinking Big, The Magic of Believing, Acres of Diamonds,* and *How to Be Rich* by J. Paul Getty. I read these books and said, "This is not what the world is telling me, but this is what I need to know. I need to know how winners think, not how average people think." They are helping me by making me understand something about myself that empowers me! Without heroes, we're all plain people, and we don't know how far we can go. So Birdie and I picked heroes. J. Paul Getty, W. Clement Stone, Moses, and Jesus are some of my heroes.

Those who can help you are not going to if you don't do your part. Is a teacher going to come over and help you for free when they assign homework but you won't do it? You're not passing. You're not putting out.

If you're going to build your own business, you need to expand your thinking. You need to read books that make you think bigger. How many books? I don't know. How many tapes? I don't know. All of us either learn from the experience of others or we have to experience it all ourselves.

Birdie and I have spent 38 years helping people change their lives, but we've found that the moment they get focused on some area other than what they are being taught, confusion comes in. So pick your mentors and pick them well; look at the ones that have had long-term success. It's a big difference between long-term success and something that's a mess. If you plan to win, learn from the best. If you plan to lose, learn from the rest. You'll know when your head rises above the crowd and you get all the tomatoes...learn to love tomato juice.

> **So pick your mentors and pick them well; look at the ones that have had long-term success.**

Isn't it funny how successful people copy each other, and they think a lot along the same lines? The same thing goes with losers. But when you stop and think about it, how come a guy like Will Rogers has been copied so many times and your neighbors haven't been copied at all? There are a lot less winners in this world and there are a lot more losers. And if you're going to become a winner, then you had better realize that you're going to join an elite crowd. You're not joining the masses.

Some of the greatest people in the world go down in life, but not in history, because they made wrong decisions.

Some of the people who seem to have the least potential grow in life, and go down in history because they made right decisions. They made a decision to pay the price and think like a winner regardless of the consequences.

You've got to accept the fact that you've got genius ability. Your mind is a muscle, and it's going to put out what you put in. If you put in garbage, then you're going to get garbage coming out. If you hang around people who have genius, then you'll be planting the seeds of genius in your mind.

For years I've had people want to rub my arm so maybe it will rub off. I said, "No, all you're going to get is sweat." You'll get the seeds of genius by hanging around the super successful people. I don't want poverty thinking. I want genius thinking.

> You've got to accept the fact that you've got genius ability.

If you're going to be successful, then you're going to start relating with people who are successful. You're going to disregard what you don't like about them, and you're going to find what you do like about them. You're going to say, "They're like me. I'm like them. I can make it okay." So many, many times today we listen to the losers instead of the winners. There may be ten thousand losers out there to tell you it won't work. Listen to the one winner who says, "You can be anything that you choose to be." The Bible says, "As a man believeth in his heart, so is he."

I've got a whole bunch of friends in books. The authors of the books I read say, "You can make it." Unfortunately, most of my friends told me I wasn't going to make it. I still loved them, but I didn't accept that prejudice against me. You cannot accept that. You've got to be prejudiced enough to say maybe I'm not good enough yet, but I'm going to get better. Remember, every winner was once judged as a loser by the ones they thought were most qualified, their friends. They're not talent scouts. Only winners can spot a winner.

When I went to the presidential inauguration in 1980, I had several people tell me that you don't go to the inauguration in cowboy boots. I got there and Reagan was wearing them. In fact, a whole lot of private jets were coming in with a bunch of

> **When you're with winners, you get dreams. When you're with losers, you get regrets.**

guys wearing cowboy boots. Average people don't know what winners do. They don't understand what is acceptable.

When you're with winners, you get dreams. When you're with losers, you get regrets. Who will you want to be with? Where do you want to go? You've got to be a fighter. If you only want acceptance, you're going to be accepted by the losers and never by the winners. The winners are the ones who pay the price. The winners are the ones that people shoot at all the time.

"I don't want to live the life my Mom and Dad did." "I want to make that change." How many of you have said that? I know I did. It doesn't make any difference if you're talking to a dentist, a doctor, a lawyer, or any other professional. Most people who are successful are the first one in their family to be successful. They changed the course for their generation. Somewhere along the line that kid said, "I want to be like those people. And I'll take the ridicule and I'll take the laughter. But I want to be there. I'm going to believe more in my dreams than in my surroundings because my dreams will become my surroundings." And they found happiness.

The winners are always part of the answer. The loser is always part of the problem. The winner always has a program. The loser always has an excuse. The winner says, "Let me do it for you." The loser says, "That's not my job." The winner sees an answer for every problem. The loser sees a problem for every answer. Your choice is, which one do you want to be?

You've got to believe more than the rest of the world; you've got to have the picture of the reality of your future. Things don't just happen, somebody makes them happen. While we were going through this dream night after night, challenge after challenge, we heard people make excuses. We learned a long time ago to accept people in spite of their excuses, but reject the excuse. If we accept their excuses, then we may have them rub off on us. We've got to realize there are two kinds of people—winners and losers.

Most rich people were poor once and didn't like it. We've been poor once, but we did something about it. The ones who are waiting for somebody else to do it for them aren't going to get it done. It's just not going to happen. Rich people

**The winners are always part of the answer. The loser is always part of the problem.**

aren't going to make poor people rich. However, in the United States of America, people on welfare are in the top two percent standard of living in the world. We don't have poverty in America. We have poverty thinking.

What's happened with Birdie's and my life, you can have happen to you, or you can follow the losers. The winners stick together. I mean, I meet winners, and the next thing I know, we have a bonding because we traveled the same road. It doesn't make any difference whether or not we'd been through the same crap that they went through, but we all came out on top!

**If you're going to be successful, then you're going to start relating with people who are successful.**

Get around the "magic." See, there are a lot of people who have energy and they've got the contacts but they don't have that magic. The magic isn't held by a lot of people. You want to get somebody working closely with you that's got that magic that makes a difference. Now, how much magic do you have? You haven't got the magic? Unless you associate with somebody who's got it, it's hard for it to rub off on you all by itself.

First we have to begin to think, and then we have to learn to think right.
**– Dexter Yager**

Thinking is the hardest work there is and that is why so few people engage in it.
**– Henry Ford**

The significant problems we face in life cannot be solved at the same level of thinking we were at when we created them.
**– Albert Einstein**

There's very little difference in people. But that little difference makes a big difference. The little difference is attitude. The big difference is whether it is positive or negative.

**– W. Clement Stone**

Things turn out best for those who make the best of the way things turn out.

**- John Wooden**

A wise man makes his own decisions, and ignorant man follows the public opinion.

**- Chinese Proverb**

# Chapter 9

## A big mouth shows a small mind

Even a fool is thought wise if he keeps silent,
and discerning if he holds his tongue.
**- Proverbs**

There are people who are always going to be picking on you. There'll always be some jerk picking on you, and then there'll be somebody else loving you. Sometimes you think the one that loves you is picking on you. And sometimes you think the one that's picking on you loves you. But you've got to understand the difference. The one that loves you is always trying to help you multiply your dream. And the one, sometimes you think that's loving you, is maybe feeling sorry for you and trying to talk you into slowing down. They're the wrong one. When you allow other people's words to stop you, they will.

You need to consider the source before considering others' opinions. What I'm trying to say is that before you can consider taking advice from someone, look at their life and see if their advice is worth following. Is their garden growing or just growing weeds? Many times, I wish that people would have to show a statement of their net worth before they're able to share their opinion.

I despise the guys who criticize and minimize the enterprise of the other guys whose enterprise has made them rise above the guys who criticize.

We've got to learn how to deal with rejection, smile and be nice. Show the beautiful smile and think, "You'll eat them words, you sucker. You don't know, man. You don't know how much rejection turns me on. I hate to lose."

The first and great commandment about critics is: Don't let them scare you. Charles Dodgson said, "If you limit your actions in life to things that nobody could possibly find fault with, you will not do much." Nothing significant has ever been accomplished without controversy, without criticism.

**A successful man is one who can lay a firm foundation with the bricks that others throw at him.**

If you are going to be successful, you're going to become a very controversial person. You're not going to be accepted by everybody. All great ideas create conflict, battle, war.

It's a well-known fact among massage therapists that they can feel whether the person is giving them positive/negative energy when they massage them. If they're working on a negative person they'll feel loss of energy, and when they're working on positive people they feel positive energy. Now, it's interesting...if you want to succeed in all things, attitude is vital, more vital than you'll ever know. I believe in the power of seeds. We plant negative seeds; we're going to have a bad crop. We plant positive seeds; we're going to have positive crop.

Success is an attitude! If people keep telling you their problems, they've got an attitude problem. If you've got a good attitude, you overcome the problem. See, first thing, if you are going to succeed you have got to have a B-I-G dream!! Dream so big that you make mountains out of molehills. The problem is that so many people have a molehill of a dream and a mountain of a problem and what you have got to do is switch it around. You have got to have a mountain of an attitude. You've got to shrink all the problems down into molehills. You've got to take care of what is most important first. You've got to have direction in where you're going. And I'll tell you something, you either stand for something, or you stand for nothing.

Do you know who the most prejudiced people in the world are? Your friends. They'll tell you everything that's wrong about you. You know what? You don't **If you are afraid of criticism, you'll die doing nothing.** need to be around them. "Satan's favorite entry into your life is usually through those closest to you" (Mike Murdock). You need to be around people who think you're great.

If you want success, you'd better keep the faith. If anybody tries to steal your faith, get away from them.

Dennis Wholey warned, "Expecting the world to treat you fairly because you are a good person is a little like expecting a bull not to attack you because you are a vegetarian." I agree with Fred Allen when he said, "If criticism had any real power to harm, the skunk would have been extinct by now." Critics, while throwing mud, are simultaneously losing ground.

Fear of criticism is the kiss of death in the courtship of achievement. Those who can—do. Those who cannot—

criticize. You can usually determine the caliber of a man by ascertaining the amount of opposition it takes to discourage him. Those who complain about the way the ball bounces are often the ones who dropped it. You can always tell a failure by the way he criticizes success. Small minds are the first to criticize large ideas. If your head sticks up above the crowd, expect more criticism than bouquets. If you are afraid of criticism, you'll die doing nothing. Don't mind the fellow who belittles you; he's only trying to cut you down to his size. A successful man is one who can lay a firm foundation with the bricks that others throw at him. If it were not for the doers, the critics would soon be out of business. Love your enemies, but if you really want to make them mad, ignore them completely.

**One thing you got to always remember, anybody who's not into edification is into division. Anyone who is into division is not into multiplication.**

When I first started building my business I dealt with all kinds of rejection, people laughing at me, ridiculing me. They said, "How could you be a winner?" "After all, we know you." See, the hardest thing for anybody to realize is that to become a success, the first step you've got to take is stepping over a lot of your friends who are laying traps for you. Most people will tell you that'll never work...whatever it is. Guess what? If they believe it won't, it won't for them. There isn't a person here who, if they're going to live a full life, won't go through a lot of criticism. And the hardest thing in the world to understand is that to catch this dream you must deal with the rejection of your dream by others you care about. Oh, they believed in all the fairy tales. They believed in the Wizard of Oz, Santa Claus, Easter Bunny, Big Foot...but not in YOU.

If you tell me who you hang out with, I'll tell you who you are. I agree with the old adage, "Those who lie down with dogs will rise up with fleas." It is always "Better to make a weak man your enemy than your friend" (Josh Billings). Those who do not respect your dream will not respect your convictions either.

> **If you tell me who you hang out with, I'll tell you who you are.**

The good news is that rejection many times is what gets you tough enough to win. When you get tired of hearing them say, "Who do you think you are? You'll never make it. It'll never happen," that's when you smile and you walk away and you say, "I'm going to smoke you, baby. You're going to eat those words."

One thing you've got to always remember—anybody who's not into edification is into division. Anyone who is into division is not into multiplication. We're going to have to divide ourselves from those who are trying to divide us because we're into multiplication. Whenever you've got division, nothing good happens. "We" makes "me" stronger. So spend time with people who are for you, not against you.

There's nobody in the world who could hurt me as much as the ones that I love the most. Strangers don't bother me, but you know what's sad about some people is that strangers bother them more than the ones that love them the most.

I went to Johnny Williams' house after he'd been in

business about six months. He started with strangers and had success. Then he went to college, and his first month in college he had even more success, again with strangers. Okay. He asked me to come out and meet his folks outside Chicago at Christmastime. So Birdie and I went out the day after Christmas. Drove out there, we were broke. We were just beginning in business, but having some success.

I'll never forget talking to his dad about the business and standing on the back porch of Johnny's house and this guy goes by in, I'll never forget, a gray flannel jogging suit. He goes, "Hey Johnny, how you doing?" And I'm saying with my mouth wide open, "That's Paul Harvey." "Yeah, I told you he lives on the street. Over across the street is the owner of Motorola," Johnny reminded me. Well, he lived in a town I had

> **Broke friends think I'm stupid and rich people think I'm a genius. Who am I going to listen to?**

never heard of. He was in a little community outside Chicago that was the wealthiest suburb in America at that time, River Forest, Illinois. His folks' friends were all millionaires. His brother-in-law was there, and he was a cocky guy. So his father introduced me to him and had us sitting in the living room, and this guy was hammering me to death with his opinions. But, I just stood my ground and treated him with great respect. I was trying to be nice to the guy. Then he says, "Well, you don't have the education, you don't have this." I said, "But you know what? I'm going to keep on fighting, and I will have it. I will be there. I will have a big business." And he kept going on and on. "I'm a doctor, son. I've got an education. I don't need it." And I confidently replied, "This is a chance to multiply."

Birdie and I left the house, and we went back to our hotel. Johnny came over and couldn't believe we were staying at that dump. He said, "Well, your business is successful?" I said, "Johnny, we don't want to put a whole bunch of money in rented space. We're here for a couple days. I'd rather buy something, and put it on my house than spend more money for motel rooms. We need a bedroom and a bathroom. We're not buying this place, we're only renting it." So Johnny said, "Dad's getting in." I said, "What?" He said, "He loves the way you beat the crap out of my cocky brother-in-law. He loved your stand. He just wants to get in and enforce you." Then anybody his dad and mom invited showed up. I remember his mother saying, "We're going to have a policy." And I'll never forget this. She said, "Any of our friends, when we invite them to meetings, are either getting in or they're off our social list." I'm going, "I've never heard this before." Everybody else is asking me, "What do my friends think?" But see, I started understanding the power of wealth thinking. They weren't worried what somebody else thought. Big men don't laugh at big ideas.

I thought, I go back to Rome, New York, and all the kids I grew up with are laughing at me and they think I'm stupid. Now I go here to River Forest, Illinois, and every one of these guys are multimillionaires, and they think I'm a genius. Broke friends think I'm stupid and rich people think I'm a genius. Who am I going to listen to? See, who are you going to let empower you? Do you want successful people to empower you, and help you have the kind of lifestyle they have? Or do you want broke people to teach you how to be broke? The Bible says, "You'll know them by their fruit." If there's no fruit there, they're fruits.

I don't know about you, but, you know, a winner takes a challenge. He lives on a dream and goes for the challenge. And when somebody says you can't do it, baby, most winners are nice, quiet guys, and they don't get in a fight or an argument there. They go out and fight to build their dreams. And then they just keep moving on in life. See, it's how you handle things that make the difference.

Back when you were a kid in school and some bully came out and punched you, did you cry? Didn't matter how much it hurt. I knew if I cried, he'd whip the crap out of me, and he'd chase me the rest of my life. If you let these bullies verbally whip you, you're dead. Every time somebody beats somebody up that I'm trying to help, I try to reinforce them and strengthen them. But if he quits, I'd let him know he was being a traitor, in a nice way, to his family and kids. Now that's his choice, but to me, this is my only chance, and this is your only chance to really be the hero you can be. Now I love people whether they quit or go on. It won't make any difference to me, but it will make a difference in their life.

All winners understand we get beat up on a regular basis, but we take our lumps and go on. All of us who have built a business discover that the bigger we build it, the more crap we go through. We went someplace new, and we kept moving. And we don't live on the hurts of the past; we live on the dreams of the future.

Unfortunately, most people will be back on their jobs, back to work again, back dealing with the average people.

The ones who gave up; the ones who have all the answers and none of the success; the ones with the wise mouth and the slow brain.

Ninety-nine percent of the people always told me what I couldn't do. Very few people, if anybody, ever told me what I could do. Even some of the ones who saw that I might succeed, made statements like, "Well, Dexter, with your limited vocabulary, limited education, who'll even want to know you when you make it?"

Winners recognize winners. Losers never recognize winners; every time they identify you as a loser. They say, "You're a loser. You'll never make it." And you've got to look and say, "They don't look like winners to me. They're not at all what I want to be. So if they think I'm a loser, they've been looking in the mirror too much and they think I'm like them."

I noticed that highly successful people don't run around telling everybody, "You're a loser. You're a loser." The most highly successful people I know are always going around saying, "You can do it. Hey, you can make it."

> I despise the guys who criticize and minimize the enterprise of the other guys whose enterprise has made them rise above the guys who criticize.

See, along the line when you start to want to achieve more, somebody will try to steal your dream, and they'll tell you what's wrong. You know, I have a burgundy book and that book is my business guide, and it's called the Holy Bible. It says God hates laziness. God talks about performance (you know, fruit and works). Now who should I believe, God or the ones that want to make the new rules? See somewhere along the line you've got to decide. If I want to fix me, then I go back to the manufacturer to get the tips.

Remember this, if you are afraid of criticism, you will die doing nothing. If you want a place in the sun, you will have to expect some blisters and some sand kicked in your face. Criticism is a compliment when you know what you're doing is right.

There's no easy road to success, folks. If you want to succeed you got to learn to get hit and stay on your feet. So many people are looking for the easy way to success. Real success is built on you getting tough. You understand that? If somebody laughing at you is going to stop you in your dream, what's going to stop you in anything else that you do too? There's always somebody laughing at you. So What! See, I have learned, let them laugh because I'm going to win.

It is not the critic who counts; not the man who points out how strong man stumbles, or where the doer of deeds could have done them better. The credit belongs to the man who is actually in the arena; whose face is marred by dust and sweat and blood; who strives valiantly; who errs and comes short again and again; who knows the great enthusiasms, the great devotions, and spends himself in a worthy cause; who, at best, knows in the end the triumph of high achievement and who, at the worst, if he fails, at least fails while daring greatly, so that his place shall never be with those cold and timid souls who know neither victory nor defeat.
- **Theodore Roosevelt**

Words kill, words give life; they're either poison or fruit—you choose.
- **Proverbs 18:21**

Remember, if people talk behind your back,
it only means you're two steps ahead.
- **Fannie Flag**

# Chapter 10

## Don't let your studies interfere with your education

*A man with an experience is never at the mercy of a man with a theory.*
**- Dexter Yager**

It's very important that we understand education—the right education. I've got nothing against education, but I do have something against bad education. Much of what's in the school system and the colleges is bad education.

> It's kind of like the man that said, "When I first got married, I had no kids and four theories. Now I have four kids and no more theories."

When I talk about education, remember that I am an educator myself. I'm not against education—I'm against the wrong kind of education. It's a sad point in America when we put so much emphasis on education and so little on experience. I've used an expression for years—listen to it and remember it well. It's a really simple statement: "A man with an experience is never at the mercy of a man with a theory." You can't disagree with it, and if you do, you're wrong, plain and simple. It's kind of like the man that said, "When I first got married, I had no kids and four theories. Now I have four kids and no more theories." Always continue learning in the school of experience, and make sure class is never out.

What is knowledge worth? It's priceless. Priceless! The

dumbest thing in the world is somebody who's not smart enough to understand the value of proven knowledge. You should never argue with a multimillionaire in his field—he's a proven champ. I always laugh because you go to share the dream to some little Joe, and he's got a clunker in the driveway. He's living in a rented apartment. Old furniture in the house, and he knows everything. But you've got to learn to be ladies and gentlemen. You can't say the old adage, "If you're so smart how come you aren't rich?" He's not even at a place where he can understand that. He just thinks he knows everything, so you've got to love him. Get him to do a little—maybe one step at a time he'll gain faith.

I don't sit around and argue with people about my business anymore. I state the facts. If they don't like it, I go find somebody who's a winner. I don't have time to mess with losers. There was a time, when I first got started when I was immature and I'd sit in the living room and argue all night with someone who was stupid. Now I just say, "Well, if that's how you feel, it's up to you." The only time I don't say that to a guy is if I see desire, action, and a willingness to learn. However, I'm willing to argue with someone who is growing and wants to keep growing, because he's worthy of the argument. He's already shown the commitment. He's just not knowledgeable enough. I'll argue with him to win my point, so he doesn't go on being wrong the rest of his life. It's very important to understand that.

Another famous saying says: "It's what you learn after you know it all that counts." I must admit that I am somewhat of a fanatic about this. I hate to have idle time—time in which I am not learning anything. Those around me know that I must always have something to read or to write during any idle moment that might arise. In fact, I try to learn from everyone. From one person I may learn what to do, while from another I might learn what not to do. One of the best teachers is other people's experience. Learn from the mistakes of others—you can never live life long enough to make all the mistakes yourself.

> **I had to dream and dream and dream. I had to stretch and stretch and stretch...**

The reason old sayings are old sayings is because they're common sense. That's why they've lasted through years. If college is so great, why do they have so many financial troubles? Well, for one, they're not graduating people to super wealth time after time, so that they can give back a few grants. Colleges are looking for the government to fund them. The government isn't that smart.

How important is experience? People will pay thirty thousand dollars to send their kids to college for one year, at some of the finest colleges, and yet most of them will never find the information in this book. Who's getting ripped off? To come from being a poor guy in the alley, a stutterer who barely graduated, to where I am today, I had to change and change and change and change. I had to dream and dream and dream. I had to stretch and stretch and stretch and gather proven knowledge every step of the way.

I'm not here to follow the world. I've got the world following me. Have you got the world following you, or are you following the world? Are you following the guys who don't know where they're going, or are you going to take the guys who don't know where they're going and lead them in the right direction?

The other day I sat down with a man who was relatively new in business. He went to college as a free enterpriser, but he came out of college as a socialist. In four years they had undone everything his dad had done in 18. He came to me and said, "Dexter, I feel I'm getting screwed up. I want to talk to you. Why this? Why that?" You see, right then he could decide to argue; instead he decided to listen and learn. Afterwards he said, "That was worth a million dollars for me to spend this afternoon with you, because I was headed toward being screwed up. I had not learned. I've got the title. I've got the lifestyle, but I have not learned all the basics, so consequently I didn't understand why. When you don't have the 'why,' somebody can knock your block off."

> **If it's on the wall and it's not in you, then you've got nothing.**

As you learn more about the free enterprise system and how it works, you're going to go out amongst a whole bunch of people who have grown up with "education" being the answer. Education is the answer, but only the right education.

The answer is not simply having a diploma on the wall. There's something wrong in most of the educational systems that drives people to the point of creating status out of a piece of paper. There's a difference between having knowledge in your head that will make you produce and become more successful and having a piece of paper. Whenever you're in an area where you can get enough education that will make you use that thing you've got called a brain better than the guy next to you so you can pass him, then that education is worth it. If it's on the wall and it's not in you, then you've got nothing.

**There are people who don't understand me and never will, because they don't study me.**

Are you going to let college education be the thing that holds you back or helps you out? You know what college mostly is? College is a whole bunch of people who have studied a whole bunch of stuff, but that doesn't mean they know anything. You don't have any real knowledge until you've performed and produced.

One of the big magazines wrote that Henry Ford was an idiot, so he sued them. They took him to court to prove that he was an idiot because he couldn't read or write. They had him "up against a wall," and they were really beating him to death in court.

**Everybody wants a lifestyle change. Everybody wants financial change, but they refuse to change themselves.**

Right in the middle of all of that he turned to the lawyer and said, "Sir, granted, I admit I can't read or write, but I can pay enough money, and you'll come to work for me to do my reading and writing. So now who's the idiot?"

There's nothing sadder than an economics professor who is broke. There's nothing sadder than economics students that stay broke. My daughter went to college for one year, and one of the classes she took was economics. She said, "Dad, I couldn't listen to that economics professor any longer. He always disagreed with you, and on top of that, he was broke." Unfortunately, that's usually the story. She said, "I don't need the degree as bad as I'm going to need the money. You can learn more in an hour with someone who has succeeded in life than you'll ever learn with a guy who's only studied life."

There are people who don't understand me and never will, because they don't study me. If you want to know me, study me. Do you want to know my wife Birdie? Study Birdie. Do you want a good marriage? Study your mate. Quit trying to change him or her. Change yourself. You're not going to change them. Everybody wants a lifestyle change. Everybody wants financial change, but they refuse to change themselves. You've got to be willing to do whatever it takes. When you're looking for somebody to teach you, you want to make sure you're looking at somebody who's developing champions. If I go down to the gym in Charlotte, North Carolina, I don't have to check a guy's qualifications to find out if he's capable of teaching me how to work out. All I've got to do is look at him. He doesn't have to be nine feet tall to make me respect him. If he's only four feet tall and he's built with muscles all over the place, I'm going to say, "Hey, this guy knows what he's doing," but if he's a ninety-eight pound weakling and he's saying, "Let me tell you how you work out with this stuff," I'm not listening. Well, why do people spend so much time listening to the guy with that same mentality when it comes to finances?

People who succeed listen and learn. They develop a great amount of faith because they learn to live on faith.

They learn to live when others are laughing at them. They see a lifestyle. They see a purpose. They see that what they are rendering is a genuine service to people, and they're willing to give it their all.

Always speak less than you know around people with more success than you. Recently I saw a sign under a mounted largemouth bass. It read: "If I had kept my mouth shut I wouldn't be here." How true! When you argue, it's hard to listen. When you talk too much, you don't hear right. And when you don't hear right, you don't learn.

> Quit getting hung up on education, and if you have too much or too little of it. Instead, start getting hung up on experience.

It's really important to understand that so many people get hung up on a degree, and then once they get it, all they do with it is hang it up. Instead, I recommend you go out and make your life a success, and then if you want a Masters Degree, just take a piece of paper and write "Masters Degree in ———," put it in a frame, and hang it on the wall. It will have more value and cost you less.

Don't feel bad because you've got a bunch of old dumb friends who are highly intelligent and are trying to make you feel stupid. They said Einstein was stupid, didn't they? A lot of people were stupid. You can read in all the books that are taught in school about how the guys were put down, but they changed history. How about changing your history first?

The highest paid people in the world are the ones who have the most experience and provide the highest value.

So how do you get experience? From mistakes or from doing things, period. Sometimes you do things right accidentally, but you've got to learn from the good mistakes and the bad mistakes.

Quit getting hung up on education, and if you have too much or too little of it. Instead, start getting hung up on experience. Experience is the key that divides the winners from the losers. It's not what somebody else says could happen, it's what you know can happen by being out there and producing.

You can lead a boy to college, but you can't make him think.
**- Elbert Hubbard**

To be upset over what you don't have is to waste what you do have.
**- Ken Keyes, Jr.**

# Chapter 11

## Mentors and Protégés

If I have seen farther than others, it is because I have stood on the shoulders of giants. **- Sir Isaac Newton**

If you want success, you're going to have to find a mentor. I was talking to a guy named Gary in the gym the other day. Gary's 51 years of age and he's been bodybuilding for 20 years. Now we're all bodybuilders, first off. You have a fat body, a skinny body, a muscular body, but we've all got bodies. It's a matter of how you want it to look. If you want to shape it, you've got to find somebody that can teach you how to shape your body. My trainer tells me, "Go look at the trainer. If they don't look like something that you want to look like, don't hire them."

Understand who your mentor is. Who do you want to get in your head?

There are no excuses. Winners do it in spite of everything. This is what everyone must learn to be the protégé.

Pick your mentors and pick them well. Look at the ones who have had long-term success. There's a big difference between long-term success and something that's a mess. You've got to have goals, and you need somebody to help stretch your goals.

One of the greatest teachers of wisdom is Mike Murdock. His books are a great source of knowledge and they've had a powerful impact on my life, and I encourage people to get his books, read them, and re-read them. In his book,

*The Wisdom Commentary 1*, Mike Murdock wrote one of the most accurate passages on the relationship between mentors and protégés that I've ever read. In fact, it is so valuable that I asked my friend Mike if I could share an excerpt from the book over the next couple of pages:

"Mentors are trusted teachers.

Various teachers will enter and exit your life. The Holy Spirit is your dominant and most important Mentor of all (see Jn. 14:15, 16).

Wisdom determines the success of your life. There are two ways to receive wisdom: mistakes and mentors.

Mentors are the difference between poverty and prosperity; decrease and increase; loss and gain; pain and pleasure; deterioration and restoration.

1. An uncommon Mentor is the Master Key to the Success of a Protégé. "Wisdom is the principal thing." (Prov. 4:7).

2. An Uncommon Mentor Transfers Wisdom Through Relationship. "He that walketh with wise men shall be wise: but a companion of fools shall be destroyed," (Prov. 13:20). Joshua knew this. "And Joshua the son of Nun was full of the spirit of Wisdom; for Moses had laid his hands upon him," (Deut. 34:9).

3. An Uncommon Mentor Guarantees Your Promotion. "Exalt her, and she shall promote thee: she shall bring thee to honour, when thou dost embrace her. She shall give to thine head an ornament of grace: a crown of glory shall she deliver to thee," (Prov. 4:8, 9).

4. An Uncommon Mentor Can Determine Your Wealth. "Riches and honour are with me; yea, durable riches and righteousness," (Prov. 8:18)

5. An Uncommon Mentor Can Paralyze Your Enemies Against You. "For I will give you a mouth and wisdom, which all your adversaries shall not be able to gainsay or resist" (Lk. 21:15).

6. An Uncommon Mentor Can Cause Influential People to Listen to You. "And Joshua the son of Nun was full of the spirit of Wisdom; for Moses had laid his hands upon him: and the children of Israel hearkened unto him..." (Deut. 34:9).

7. An Uncommon Mentor Will Require Your Pursuit. He does not need what you know. You need what he knows. Elijah never pursued Elisha. Elisha desired what was in him. The proof of desire is pursuit.

8. An Uncommon Mentor is More Interested In your Success Than Your Affection. His focus is not the celebration of you, but the correc-

tion of you.

9. An Uncommon Mentor Is Not Necessarily Your Best Friend:

• Your best friend loves you the way you are. Your mentor loves you too much to leave you the way you are.

• Your best friend is comfortable with your past. Your mentor is comfortable with your future.

• Your best friend ignores your weakness. Your mentor removes your weakness.

• Your best friend is your cheerleader. Your mentor is your coach.

• Your best friend sees what you do right. Your mentor sees what you do wrong.

10. A Mentor Sees Things You Cannot See. He sees weaknesses in you before you experience the pain of them. He sees an enemy before you discern him. He has already experienced the pain of a problem you are about to create.

11. An Uncommon Mentor Will Become an Enemy to the Enemies of his Protégé. Jesus proved this. "Simon, Simon, behold Satan hath desired to have you, that he may sift you as wheat: But I have prayed for thee, that thy faith fail not: and when thou art converted, strengthen thy brethren," (Lk. 22:31, 32). An Uncommon Mentor will fight against any philosophy, pitfalls, or prejudices that would rob the protégé of experiencing complete success in his life.

12. An Uncommon Mentor can Create An Uncommon Protégé. Jesus took Peter, a fisherman, and turned him into a master preacher. Everything you know will come through mentorship, by experience, or through a person.

Invest everything to spend time and moments with the Uncommon Mentor God has chose to sow into your life.

A protégé is an obedient learner.

The wisdom of the mentor is perpetuated through the protégé. True success will produce a successor. Jesus took twelve protégés and revolutionized the Earth. It is very important that you recognize those connected to you by the Holy Spirit for the multiplying and perpetuation of your success and life.

You will only remember what you teach another. Our children should become our protégés.

Passive Protégés only reach when it is convenient, or when their personal efforts do not produce their desired result. They subconsciously expect their mentor to produce success for them.

Parasite Protégés pursue for credibility, not correction. They will use the name and influence of a mentor to manipulate others into a relationship. They want what the mentor has earned, not what he has learned. They want reputation without preparation.

Prodigal Protégés enter and exit the relationship freely. When serious correction occurs, they move toward another mentor who has not yet discovered their flaws. They distance themselves when their mentor encounters personal difficulties, loss of credibility, or false accusation or persecution. They only return when their pigpen becomes unbearable.

Productive Protégés are Uncommon. They have a servant's heart. They never make a major decision without the counsel and feedback of their mentor. They view their mentor as a dominant gift from God. They love their mentor as much as themselves.

The Uncommon Protégé assigned by God will honor the mentor. "And we beseech you, brethren, to know them which labour among you, and are over you in the Lord, and admonish you; And to esteem them very highly in love for their work's sake," (1 Thess. 5:12, 13).

1. The Uncommon Protégé Will Invest Everything To Stay in the Presence of the Uncommon Mentor. Ruth persisted. "Entreat me not to leave thee, or to return from following after thee: for whither thou goest, I will go:" (Ruth 1:16).

2. The Uncommon Protégé Follows The Counsel for the Uncommon Mentor. God established the punishment of a rebellious protégé who sneered at the counsel of his covering. "And the man that will do presumptuously, and will not hearken unto the priest that standeth to minister there before the Lord thy God, or unto the judge, even that man shall die: and thou shalt put away the evil from Israel. And all the people shall hear, and fear, and do no more presumptuously," (Deut. 17:12, 13).

3. The Uncommon Protégé Reveals the Secrets and Dreams of his Heart With the Mentor. Ruth opened her heart to Naomi. Elisha expressed his longings to Elijah. Vulnerability creates the unbreakable bond between a Mentor and the protégé.

4. Then Uncommon Protégé Freely Discusses His Mistakes And Pain With The Mentor. David did. "So David fled, and escaped, and came to Samuel to Ramah, and told him all that Saul had done to him. And he and Samuel went and dwelt in Naioth" (1 Sam 19:18).

5. The Uncommon Protégé Defines Clearly His Expectations to the Mentor. Elisha explained his desire to Elijah. Ruth explained her desire to Naomi.

6. The Uncommon Protégé Gladly Sows Seeds Of Appreciation Back into the Life of the Mentor. It was the secret of the queen of Sheba. She presented over four million dollars of gifts when she met Solomon for the appointment. "And she came to Jerusalem with a very great train, with camels that bare spices, and very much gold, and precious stones: and when she was come to Solomon, she communed with him of all that was in her heart. And Solomon told her all her questions: there was not any thing hid from the king, which he told her not...And she gave the king a hundred and twenty talents of gold, and of spices very great store, and precious stones: there came no more such abundance of spices as these which the queen of Sheba gave to king Solomon," (1 Kings 10:2, 3, 10).

The remarkable mentor, the Apostle Paul, received such gifts. "For even in Thessalonica ye sent once and again unto my necessity," (Phil. 4:16).

7. The Uncommon Protégé Ultimately Receives the Mantle of The Mentor He Serves. Transference of anointing is a fact, not a fantasy. The Apostle Paul documented it. "Wherefore I put thee in remembrance that thou stir up the gift of God, which is in thee by the putting on of my hands," (2 Tim. 1:6).

8. The Uncommon Protégé Moves Toward the Shelter of the Mentor During a Season of Uncommon Attack and Warfare. The picture of David and Samuel's relationship is remarkable. "So David fled, and escaped, and came to Samuel to Ramah, and told him all that Saul had done to him. And he and Samuel went and dwelt in Naioth," (1 Sam. 19:18). Think about this seriously. During serious attack, David did not withdraw from Samuel. He pursued him. He invested time with him.

9. The Uncommon Protégé Will Change his Own Schedule To Invest Time In The Presence of the Mentor. Paul did. "Neither went I up to Jerusalem to them which were apostles before me; but I went into Arabia, and returned again unto Damascus. Then after three years I went up to Jerusalem to see Peter, and abode with him fifteen days," (Gal. 1:17, 18).

The Uncommon Protégé is someone who discerns, respects, and pursues the answers God has stored in the mentor for his or her life."

Chapter 11

> **The higher you go in life, the more dependent you will become on other people.**

I go to the gym when I'm home in Stuart, Florida. I have a trainer named David who has won the Mr. Florida contest four times. He's 50 years old. I've shown his business card around, and so many women say, "You wouldn't want to look like that, would you?" He's all muscle. He's big, 5'5", weighs about 210 pounds. Like a rock. Next to the fat slob I was at 240, I'd like to have half his body. I decided eight years ago to drop eighty pounds. I did it in six months. I started a training program, worked out for four years getting different equipment, trying to understand working out, and got myself in halfway decent starting shape. Then I went and hired David. I have been working with him for four years. After all that I didn't end up a big muscular guy like him. What happened? What's wrong? First thing, I've had to reverse 55 years of stupidity. Some people get in the contest and twelve weeks later they went from a fat person to big muscular person, and they had something more to work with.

> **If you need to know, find someone in the know.**

When I go to the gym, I pay my trainer 75 bucks an hour to make me do what I don't want to do. I do everything he tells me to do. That's what you've got to do. You've got to find a mentor you trust. Learn everything you can. Make sure he knows what he's doing, follow the instructions, and ask questions.

If you need to know, find someone in the know. When I know somebody that has what I want, I go ask them how to get it. I don't expect an overnight miracle.

> **When I know somebody that has what I want, I go ask them how to get it.**

We need people that make us stretch, not people that make us fall. People that make us achieve more because we cannot believe we can do it. We've got to do it. Surround yourself with achievers, believers, and doers. If you want to win, you'd better learn to get a mentor that can teach you to win.

Behind a capable man there are always other capable men. Work together with others. Remember the banana— every time it leaves the bunch, it gets peeled and eaten. You'll never experience lasting success without relationships with people. No one person alone can match the cooperative efforts of the right team.

Having the right mentor can cause influential people to listen to you. I can't tell you how many times I have seen this happen. Just this simple connection has made a huge impact for so many people. Many times mentors are the difference between poverty and prosperity. I believe that God has divine connections for all of us.

There is no such thing as a "self-made" man. We are made up of thousands of others. The man who only works by himself and for himself is likely to be corrupted by the company he keeps. Everyone who has ever done a kind deed for us, or spoken one word of encouragement to us, has entered into the make-up of our character and of our thoughts, as well as our success. Says George Matthew Adams, "I not only use all the brains I have, but all that I can borrow."

Learn from the best and pass the rest. You want to teach people how to be a mentor. The higher you go in life, the more dependent you will become on other people. A conceited person never gets anywhere because he thinks he is already there. Every great man is always being helped by somebody.

You're smart when you realize how dumb you are. You're really smart when you know your weaknesses and your strengths. You're really stupid when you can't realize your weaknesses. Everybody needs help.

When God gets ready to bless you he sends a person into your life. God blesses people through people. With some people you spend an evening, with others you invest it. Wise is the man or woman who fortifies their life with right associations and mentors.

> He that walketh with wise men shall be wise...
> **– Proverbs 13:19-21**

> In everyone's life, at sometime, our inner fire goes out. It is then burst into flame by an encounter with another human being. We should all be thankful for those people who rekindle the inner spirit.
> **– Proverbs 13:19-21**

> As iron sharpens iron, so one person sharpens the wits of another.
> **– Proverbs 27:17**

# Chapter 12

## Major on majors

Keep the main thing the main thing.
**- Anonymous**

I've always been a flexible person, but I have a certain rule. I major on the majors, and I minor on the minors. I don't major on the minors or minor on the majors. If it's major, I handle it. And, if it's minor, I forget it.

Now, you and I have got to learn how to take the major areas of our life and force ourselves to be productive so we can be proud of ourselves and then other people around us will be proud of us. Do you have a problem? Get rid of it and let's get on with it. Get rid of your problem. See, don't hang on to it. Some of you are hanging on to a problem instead of going after a solution. See, I live on solutions. I don't live on problems. The only times that I mess with a problem is when I'm working on a solution. You give me your problem; I'll give you the solution. You see, I know because I've had to come up with all those solutions for myself. You haven't got a problem that I haven't had. I learned along the line, you'll find a few guys that create problems—they're inventors of problems. You know, if you find one guy that comes up with fifteen problems you've

> I major on the majors, and I minor on the minors.

never had before, he hasn't had those problems either. He's just trying to think up something. A real winner is hard to live with because we have principles and we lay it flat down on the line. "This is the way it is. I have had it, and this is stopping here and now, period." And my favorite saying has always been, "That's it, period." And when you hear, "That's it, period," watch out!

---

**What you set your heart on will determine how you will spend your life.**

---

Majoring in majors is all about priorities. We know what the priorities are in life. For me, they are Number 1: God; Number 2: Family; Number 3: Country; Number 4: Profession. Okay, those are your priorities in life, aren't they? God created me, created you. He made us with the potential to be the best, but it's our decision.

A major key to success is to get more on your plate than what you can do, then you start doing what has to be done. You'll stop messing around with little things, and you'll major on majors. Ninety-five percent of the people in business spend 95 percent of their time majoring on minors. With most leaders you can find a number of faults because we mess up on more little things than what you could ever believe—we've got more on our plate than we can handle. We major on majors and you see us mess up on minors and you think, "Oh my, how I can follow him!" Learn to major on majors.

If you allow minors to become majors you find yourself spread so thin that you're mediocre at everything and excellent in nothing. Do more by doing less. Delegate, simplify or eliminate low priorities as soon as possible. James Liter said, "One thought driven home is better than three left on base."

What you set your heart on will determine how you will spend your life. Follow this powerful advice from Paul the apostle who wrote, "This one thing I do...I press towards the mark." Carl Sandberg said, "There are people who want to be everywhere at once and they get nowhere."

> **A major key to success is to get more on your plate than what you can do, then you start doing what has to be done.**

One key to results is being focused. Perhaps no other key to growth and success is as overlooked as this is. The temptation is always to do a little bit of everything. "There is so little time for the discovery of all that we want to know about things that really interest us. We cannot afford to waste it on things that are only of casual concern for us, or in which we are interested only because other people have told us what we ought to be" (Alec Waugh). Without focus, there is no peace or productivity.

There will come a time in your life when you must learn to say *no* to many good ideas. In fact, the more you grow, the more opportunities you will have to say *no* to.

*Yes* and *no* are the two most important words that you will ever say. These are the two words that determine your destiny in life. How and when you say them will affect your entire future.

Decide to major in majors.

# Chapter 12

Rule number one is, don't sweat the small stuff.
Rule number two is, it's all small stuff.
**- Robert Eliot**


If you are not able to separate the critical few from the meaningless many—
then it all just becomes noise.
**- Anonymous**


If everything is a priority then nothing is a priority.
**- Stephen Covey**

# Chapter 13

## Show up!

Ninety percent of success is simply showing up.
- **Dexter Yager**

I decided years ago it was important that I showed up. Whatever condition I was in, it was going to be important that I be there. This is what makes us move from being the little man and the little woman to the big man and the big woman; from little shot to big shot; from ordinary to extraordinary.

The problem with so many people is they make so many excuses why they cannot, instead of making decisions why they can. See your life changes when you start making decisions. I can tell you my life changed when I started making a decision to show up to be there.

Here's some great news: God will use you right where you are today. You don't need to do anything else for God to begin to use you now. You don't have to read another book, listen to another audio, memorize another scripture, plant another seed gift, or repeat another creed or confession. You don't even need to attend another church service before God can use you. All you have to do is show up and begin.

Just start, because God uses willing vessels, not brimming vessels. Follow this powerful advice, "I have a simple philosophy. Fill what's empty. Empty what's full. Scratch where it itches" (Alice Roosevelt).

Everything big starts with something little. Nothing great is created suddenly. Never decide to do nothing just because you can only do a little. These kinds of decisions are major even though sometimes they seem minor at the time.

What you can do—you can do. What works? Work on that. Don't wish you could do things you cannot do. Instead, think of what you can do. Everyone who got to where he is had to begin where he was. Only one person in a thousand knows how to really live in the present. The problem is that we seldom think of what we have; instead, we think of what we lack.

"We don't need more strength or more ability or greater opportunity. What we need to use is what we have" (Basil Walsh). People are always ignoring something they can do and trying to do something they can't. Learning new things won't help the person who isn't using what he already knows. Success means doing the best we can with what we have.

> **Ninety percent of success is showing up and starting. You may be disappointed if you fail, but you are doomed if you don't try.**

Step up and step out when you have a chance to do something different or exciting with your life, even if you're scared. You live in a world of fear or you live in a world of faith. And if you want to know where things are today, the future's in the world of faith, not in the world of fear.

Here's some of the best advice I've been given: "Do something!"

The courage to begin is the same courage it takes to succeed. This is the courage that usually separates dreamers from achievers. The beginning is the most important part of any endeavor. Ninety percent of success is showing up and starting. You may be disappointed if you fail, but you are doomed if you don't try.

Don't be deceived; knowledge alone of where you want to go can never be a substitute for putting one foot in front of the other. Discover step-by-step excitement. To win you must begin.

**Everyone who got to where he is, had to begin where he was.**

Ask yourself: "If I don't take action now, what will this ultimately cost me?" When a procrastinator has finally made up his mind, the opportunity has always passed by. Edwin Markum said, "When duty comes a knocking at your gate, welcome him in; for if you bid him wait, He will depart only to come once more and bring seven other duties to your door."

Occasionally you may see someone who doesn't do anything yet seems to be successful in life. Don't be deceived. Remember the old saying, "Even a broken clock is right twice a day."

This old saying is true, "Nothing is as fatiguing as the eternal hanging on of an uncompleted task." People who delay action until all factors are perfect, do nothing. Jimmy Lyons said, "Tomorrow is the only day in the year that appeals to a lazy man."

Procrastination is the grave in which opportunity is buried. Anybody who brags about what he's going to do tomorrow probably did the same thing yesterday. Few things are more dangerous to a person's character than having nothing to do and plenty of time in which to do it. Killing time is not murder, it's suicide. Two things rob people of their peace of mind: work unfinished and work not yet begun. Yes, you must "Show Up."

---

**Two things rob people of their peace of mind: work unfinished and work not yet begun.**

---

All I did was go to work everyday.
- **Rich Devos**

# Chapter 14

## Live it, eat it, sleep it...

If you want success, learn to love what you do.
- **Dexter Yager**

Earl Nightingale said, "A young man once asked a great and famous older man, 'How can I make a name for myself in the world and become successful?' The great and famous man replied: "You have only to decide upon what it is you want and then stay with it, never deviating from your course no matter how long it takes, or how rough the road, until you have accomplished it." Success seems to be largely a matter of holding on after others have let go.

Some of the real basics of life are to learn to build your dream big-

> Persistent people begin their success where most others quit. The fact is that people don't fail; they just give up too easily.

ger, stretch your mind, plant the seeds of success in your subconscious mind and force yourself to perform without giving up. Stop and think. How many of you have excelled at something sometime during your life? All of you have, haven't you? Where did you excel? How did you do it? I'll bet you ate it, lived it and slept it, didn't you? You didn't let anything get in your way.

"The nose of the bulldog is slanted backwards so he can

continue to breathe without letting go" (Winston Churchill). Many people eagerly begin "the good fight of faith," but then forget to add patience, persistence, and endurance to their enthusiasm. Persistent people begin their success where most others quit. The fact is that people don't fail; they just give up too easily.

There were two men shipwrecked on an island. The minute they got onto the island one of them started screaming and yelling, "We're going to die! We're going to die! There's no food! No water! We're going to die!"

**It takes fewer than one half of one percent of people who are totally committed to an idea to change the way the world thinks, whether it's good or bad.**

The second man was propped up against a palm tree and acting so calmly it drove the first man crazy.

"Don't you understand? We're going to die!"

The second man replied, "You don't understand, I make one hundred thousand dollars a month."

The first man looked at him quite dumfounded and asked, "What difference does that make?!? We're on an island with no food and no water! We're going to DIE!"

The second man answered, "You just don't get it. I make one hundred thousand dollars a month and I tithe ten percent on that one hundred thousand dollars a week. My pastor will find me!"

When you are persistent, you know it and so does everyone else.

Never give up on what you really know you should do.

Failure is waiting on the path of least persistence. The "man of the hour" spent many days and nights getting there.

Consider the man who said, "My overnight success was the longest night of my life." Winners simply do what losers don't want to do any longer.

When faced with some real health challenges, I went on a diet, bought some stuff to have a gym in my house and started working out. I didn't really know what to do, but I knew I had to do something. More importantly, I had to keep on doing something, if I wanted the results I knew I needed. Just starting is never good enough. When you make a commitment to do something in life, stick to it no matter what.

> When you make a commitment to do something in life, stick to it no matter what.

It's been said that a great oak is only a little nut that held its ground. "These troubles and sufferings of ours are, after all, quite small and won't last very long. Yet this short time of distress will result in God's richest blessing upon us forever and ever" (2 Cor. 4:17). Too many take hold of opportunity, but let go of it too soon.

Christopher Morley says, "Big shots are only little shots that keep shooting." Endurance, patience, and commitment are simply a state of enjoying the distance between God's promises and provision for your life. "Endurance is patience concentrated" (Thomas Carlisle). Beware the fury of a persistent man. There's an energy to persistence. "The desire accomplished is sweet to the soul" (Proverbs 13:19).

Persistence may be bitter, but its fruit is sweet.

It takes less than one half of 1 percent of people that are totally committed to an idea to change the way the world thinks, whether it's good or bad. You can change the history of your business, your family, your finances, your friends, and American future, but only with a passionate determination.

"Enduring" is a military term meaning, "to hold up courageously under fire." You can stay in the fight when you feel like quitting by bringing more of God into that area of your life. Proverbs 16:3 NIV says, "Commit to the Lord whatever you do, and your plans will succeed." The famous saying is true, "There is no greater wealth than the wealth of commitment. It cannot be robbed from you. Only you can lose it by your will."

> Endurance, patience, and commitment are simply a state of enjoying the distance between God's promises and provision for your life.

Socrates had a boy come up and say, "I want to study under you. I want to learn from you." And he took the boy by the hand. He walked with him down into the water, and he reached down and put the boy's head under the water. The kid came up fighting, and again, Socrates forced his head under the water. Again, the boy fought back. Socrates said, "When you want to learn from me, like you wanted air, life itself, then you will be my protégé." You've got to want it bad enough. You've got to want your dream bad enough for your wife, for your kids, for your freedom, for your country, for your ministry, for your self-image. Most people don't want anything bad enough to get it. If they can get it on a credit card, then they get it, end up in debt, and they risk going bankrupt. They don't understand paying the price.

A man meets a guru in the road. The man asks the guru, "Which way is success?"

The berobed, bearded sage doesn't speak but points to a place off in the distance.

The man, thrilled by the prospect of quick and easy success, rushes off in the appropriate direction. Suddenly, there comes a loud "Splat!"

Eventually, the man limps back, tattered and stunned, assuming he must have misinterpreted the message. He repeats his question to the guru, who again points silently in the same direction.

> **Most people don't want anything bad enough to get it.**

The man obediently walks off once more. This time the splat is deafening, and when the man crawls back, he is bloody, broken, tattered, and irate. "I asked you which way is success," he screams at the guru. "I followed the direction you indicated. And all I got was splattered! No more of this pointing! Talk!"

Only then does the guru speak, and what he says is this: "Success is that way. Just a little after the splat."

All of us have experienced "the splat". It's what we do after the splat that makes all of the difference. Many times this is what separates high achievers from non-achievers. Whatever you want to accomplish in life will require persistence. Champion race car driver Rick Mears said it best, "To finish first you must first finish."

It's irritating to others when we have singleness of purpose, because most people are running around confused, not knowing what to do. It irritates them. The world makes room for a man of determination and purpose.

Faith and hope help us to be more persevering. It is something that we give to each other. It's something friends give to each other. The more we give it, the more we get. The neat part about business is that you'll find a lot of friends that think just like you. When you prove yourself enough, that relationship is there. And everybody that's somebody can tell you that they had special friends that encouraged them. They doubted, but most people doubt. You've got to get past the doubting. You're going to fall; just pick yourself up again. You've got to believe. You've got to live on faith. Listen to another audio. Read another book. Get more encouragement. Get more energy and more faith in you. Keep going until your cup runneth over. Then you will need a new dream because your cup ran over.

**Don't tell me how bad you've got it. Tell me how good you're going to get it. Don't tell me about your problems. Tell me about your dreams.**

By being persistent, every possible thing you could think of, anybody that you want to meet, you can meet. You'll find out that the more successful they are, the more they understand why you're doing what you're doing. Determination creates opportunity, your chance to go for your dreams. Your chance to change your life.

Every day I get more and more committed, more and more sold out. Don't allow yourself the luxury of a negative thought! Don't allow yourself to think anything but success! "I'm going to do it, I'll do it, and I want to make it happen."

Persistence is a decision; don't tell me your hard luck story. It's your choice. Success is a decision; struggle is just part of what you've got to go through. Don't live on your hurts; don't live on your scars, live on the stars. Keep going for the dream.

One of the hardest things for people to understand is people that live by faith. When you live by real faith, you cannot be shaken because you've chosen a dream that's bigger than all the people combined that have given you problems. We don't live on our problems; we come up with solutions. Now you've got to put your hand to it, go out, and make it happen.

Don't tell me how bad you've got it. Tell me how good you're going to get it. Don't tell me about your problems. Tell me about your dreams. Dreams are the solutions to your problems. Everybody's got something to overcome, but the joy is in overcoming it. How big is your dream today? Will you put a commitment behind the dream? Will you make it happen?

Our daily motto should be: "Have the determination of a weed." All great achievements require time and tenacity. Be persevering, because the last key on the ring may be the one that opens the door. Hanging on one second longer than your competition makes you a winner. Become famous for finishing important, difficult tasks.

When work, commitment, and pleasure all become one and you reach that deep well where passion lives, nothing is impossible.

- **Anonymous**

# Chapter 15

## The facts don't count

The mind is the limit. As long as the mind can envision the fact that you can
do something, you can do it - as long as you believe a hundred percent.
**- Arnold Schwarzenegger**

As a kid, I remember we would have Wheaties, the breakfast of champions, at the breakfast table. On the front of that box there was a champion named Bob Richards. For so many years, I saw his picture. The guy that won the "Gold Medal" for pole vaulting so many times in the Olympics. Bob Richards always said that he was a little guy that got into the Olympics. He told me that he tried out for the basketball team, but he was too short, 5'8." Coach told him he was too small and to forget about athletics. But he said that if you are going to be a champion, you've got to get the heart of the champion. He said, "I learned that if I was going to get my body over that bar, I was going to have to put my heart on the pole, throw my heart over the bar first, and my body would follow." The facts don't count when you are dealing with a winner.

> I believe we are all created equal with the right to become unequal.

I believe we are all created equal with the right to become unequal. You can be whatever you want regardless of color, race, or religion. It is up to you to develop the power of a dream and go for it. Ask somebody to help you in helping yourself. Get somebody to counsel you on how to move on your own. God gives us all a talent; it is our job to develop the talent and our dreams.

Learn to think impossible thoughts. The person with imagination beyond their present circumstances is never alone and never finished. You were created for creativity. By not being held back by "the facts", your eyes can look for opportunity, your ears will listen for direction, your mind will love a challenge and your heart will long for God's way, his designs for you. Your heart has eyes that the brain knows nothing of. Make a daily demand on your creativity.

Problems really multiply when your dreaming stops. You and I have a responsibility to feed, nurture, and develop one of the most precious things we have—our dream—to make it grow so we will grow. You can go into most gas stations, and they will laugh at your dreams; or you can be with the achievers, and they talk about their next dream. Which group do you want to be with, the dreamers or the "it won't happen, it can't work, you are crazy" group? The best education is learning from those who have gone before you.

**Your heart has eyes the brain knows nothing of.**

You have got to learn that, as a winner, the facts don't count. When you are going through something, you make up your mind that regardless of what people tell you and whatever information or facts they say that oppose you or your accomplishments, you've got to find or make up your own facts that support you and your goals. I can do it in spite of this and in spite of that and all of the rules; winners understand this. They build their own ladders to their own dreams. We looked at our old life, and we looked at what we wanted. We became the very first Dexter and Birdie impersonators because we started seeing what we wanted, and we started believing it. We started practicing new habits, saying new words, and dreaming new dreams.

It's out there for you. But it takes faith, belief, and willingness to change your paradigm. God says that if you don't believe Him, then He cannot help you. So you have to believe that He is, and that He's a rewarder of those that believe in Him.

> **You've got to decide to make a commitment, a concentrated effort that you're going to succeed no matter what the "evidence" says.**

A friend of ours is the number one cancer specialist in New York City, Park Avenue, and he specializes in pancreatic cancer. He said that 60 percent of the patients that come to him are at their last hope. They have six months to live, and he tells them how to whip cancer. The first thing they do is go home, and they tell their friends. They've got to do this, they've got to eat that, and their friends start ridiculing them. They shower them with "the facts" and more. They add to "the facts" to create an even worse "truth." What happens, they don't do it. Now think about it. Death wish. They allowed somebody else to take their life away when they'd been told how to live. So what difference does it make how many dropped out or quit? That's your choice. That's your freedom. But strong-willed people make a decision and say,

"Whatever the challenge is, I'm not putting up with that."

Not being a person of imagination causes your life to be less than it was intended to be. A dream is one of the most exciting things there is. You've got to decide to make a commitment, a concentrated effort that you're going to succeed no matter what the "evidence" says.

Aerodynamically the bumblebee shouldn't be able to fly, but the bumblebee doesn't know that so it goes on flying anyway.
**- Ed Foreman**

# Chapter 16

## If you quit you lose

There are no losers. Only winners and quitters
**- Dexter Yager**

I thank God that my dad was a winner. He worked hard. He never gave up.

One of the best blessings you can have is to be around winners and to let your kids see that you are one also by seeing things all the way through.

There's a common thread that runs through the lives of

> **Quit quitting and start starting!**

exceptional people. They have been beat up, hit on the head, knocked down, vilified, and for years they get nowhere. But every time they're knocked down, they stand up. You cannot destroy these people.

"The world will always give you the opportunity to quit, but only the world would call quitting an opportunity" (Clint Brown).

Quit quitting and start starting! Get in the habit of creating new beginnings. They give us energy, renew and revitalize our efforts. Every time we start over we begin again with far more experience and a greater chance for success than we had the last time.

When you get to the end of your rope, be thankful—God is there! The trouble with many people is that they stop faster than they started. The tragedy of life is what dies inside a man while he lives. Make this your motto: Don't die until you are dead. I remember hearing a saying years ago, "Here lives a man—died age 40—buried age 65." When was the last time you did something for the first time? "The only thing worse than a quitter is the man who is afraid to begin" (Richard Bach). Here is the test to find whether your mission on earth is finished: if you're alive, it isn't.

The only life we've got is what's left. It's up to you to make it a better quality life than you currently have. You cannot live on what it could've been. You've got to live on what it will be. The future is your choice.

**Many people who fail did not realize how close they were to success when they gave up.**

A lazy man is always judged by what he doesn't do. The more diligently we work, the harder it is to quit. Persistence is a habit—so is quitting. The choice of giving up or going on is a defining moment in your life.

**You cannot live on what it could've been. You've got to live on what it will be.**

Many people who fail did not realize how close they were to success when they gave up. "When you get into a tight place and everything goes against you, until it seems as though you could not hold on a minute longer, never give up then, for that is just the time and place that the tide will turn" (Harriet Beecher Stowe). The one thing that you've got to realize is that your real friends will encourage you and love you when you try again.

You know, people will ask you when you start doing something new or different than what the crowd is doing, "What's the dropout rate?" I'm going to tell you something. Dropout rate means absolutely nothing. If priests and rabbis and ministers were worried about dropout rate, they'd never marry anybody. The odds don't count.

> **If priests and rabbis and ministers were worried about dropout rate, they'd never marry anybody.**

Most people are professional quitters. There are places where you can buy used fitness equipment. Just about any town of any size has a place you can go. People buy it, and it sits there. It's called great intentions. If you want success, you've got to decide to be the champion of your life and your dreams.

We can become someone for our kids to believe in. Are we going to pour it on and show them what winning is all about? Or are we going to give them excuses? You've got to keep doing it. You know what the greatest reward you might have out of parenting? Your kids saw that you never quit.

I used to ask Birdie, "How does somebody fall out of love?" Love's a commitment. Love's a decision. Love isn't based on whether the guy treated you nicely today or not. That's lack of respect. You may not respect the person, but if you commit yourself to them you love them or you don't. If you don't love them, then it's because you're backing off on your commitment. In spite of what happens, God loves me period. He doesn't always like what I do, but He loves me. Aren't you glad He doesn't quit on you? Now, don't quit on Him.

I believe we have been put on this earth to be productive. The bible never talks about retirement.

God's gift is what he gives us right now. What we become is our gift back to him. We should be on the road to improvement all the days of our life because you and I are appreciative of the gift of life. We're an example to others of what they can become. It will give them hope. But if we just tell our failure story, it will not encourage them. They don't need to hear it. We don't need to tell it. We need to tell about our winning. We've got to tell them how we overcame our struggles, and then they can overcome their own.

> People of mediocre ability sometimes achieve outstanding success because they don't know when to quit. Most men succeed not because they are destined to but rather because they are determined to.
> **- George Allen**

> Whatever you do, you need courage. Whatever course you decide upon, there is always someone to tell you you are wrong. There are always difficulties arising which tempt you to believe that your critics are right. To map out a course of action and follow it to the end requires some of the same courage which a soldier needs.
> **- Ralph Waldo Emerson**

> We must build dikes of courage to hold back the flood of fear.
> **- Martin Luther King, Jr.**

> He who loses wealth loses much; he who loses a friend loses more; but he that loses his courage loses all.
> **- Miguel de Cervantess**

# Chapter 17

## Persistency: Keep on keeping on

*Nothing in the world can take the place of persistence.*
**- Calvin Coolidge**

Do you want to be successful? Are you willing to believe it without results? See, that's what separates the winners and the losers. The winners believe even when there aren't any results, and they keep plunging forward. Is it more accurate to judge your day by the harvest or the seeds you plant?

The losers keep looking for that miracle to pop out and show them they're on the right track. The winners take it one day at a time, one step at a time. Then, all of the sudden, people look and they say, "Boy you've got a big business." And the winners will look and say, "It isn't big enough yet."

When you keep on pursuing, you're building your world. And as long as you're chasing a dream, you'll deal with disappointing results. That's life. You want to talk about business or marriage or raising kids; you're going to have the same challenges. Wake up!!! You've got to go through a lot of times where it looks like nothing's happening. But, is it worth it for your husband? Is it worth it, guys, for your wife? Is it worth it for your kids? Is it worth it for you? See, most of

> **The winners believe even when there aren't any results, and they keep plunging forward.**

us who are married wouldn't be anything if we didn't have somebody special to try to be somebody special for. Isn't that right?

I'm not going to stop setting goals no matter what it looks like. Some people say, "I set that goal ten times." Well set it another ten. And if that isn't enough, set it another ten. I've reached every goal when I've set it enough times. Some of you haven't set them enough. You're only competing with your past. You're not competing with anybody else. The goal is what drives you.

The Bible says, "To everything there is a season, a time for every purpose under heaven." Every idea and dream goes through seasons. There is a winter time. That's when you get the idea, lay the foundation and almost always...nothing happens. That is followed by spring time. During spring time you plant your seed, work real hard nurturing the seed and the soil, and only a small amount of growth occurs. Then there is summer time. Summer time brings good growth, but only a limited harvest. Summer is then followed by fall. Harvest time! This is when you see the greatest results. But, sadly most people never make it to "harvest time." They give up too soon. They see no or little results and they quit right before their harvest. So, be confident and know that even though it looks like nothing is happening for you,

**Every one of us needs to have the habit of always looking ahead to where we want to go, regardless of what it looks like today.**

something is happening whether you see it or not.

When you understand that God is a God of seasons, it prepares you to do the right thing at the right time. It inspires you to persevere to the fall. God's Word is true when it says, "Let us not become weary in doing good, for at the proper time we will reap a harvest if we don't give up" (Gal 6:9NIV).

If you pluck the blossoms, you must do without the fruit.

People say, "What happened to this person? What happened to that leader?" They got out of focus, focusing on the wrong things, focusing on something temporary instead of something long term. They looked at the "drought," not the roots that were growing underground, or the rain God was sending to make their seeds grow like crazy. God wants you to have a long-term vision, long-term hopes, long-term effort, and long-term commitment. This is not fly by night. You've got to give yourself time.

I read the other day that success is not a doorway; it's a stairway taken one step at a time. And if you are afraid to take the next step, then what are you going to do? If you're not going up the stairs, then where are you going? You're going down because there is no such thing as staying where you are.

Every one of us needs to have the habit of always looking ahead to where we want to go, regardless of what it looks like today. We purposely kept looking down the road to where we wanted to be. Do you know the result of that? Every time we did that, even if things were slow, it brought another explosion. I believe a lot of it was related to the way we looked at it. We didn't dwell on what was or was not happening. We didn't keep looking at the part of life we didn't want. We kept focusing on where we wanted to go.

Success-oriented people believe enough in an ideal to hang in there until they make it. It's like planting a tree. When you plant a tree, do you give it three months or three years to grow, or are you going to cut it down?

A winner always sees more than where he's at and keeps going. A loser always sees somebody else getting the breaks and stops too soon. How much holding power do you have? It's been said that you and I should be like a postage stamp. You see, a postage stamp's usefulness consists of its ability to stick to something until it gets there.

---

**A winner always sees more than where he's at and keeps going. A loser always sees somebody else getting the breaks and stops too soon.**

---

My strength lies solely in my tenacity.
**- Louis Pasteur**

Commitment to continuity creates emotional stability.
**- Anonymous**

Nothing in the world can take the place of persistence. Talent will not; nothing is more common than unsuccessful men with talent. Genius will not; unrewarded genius is almost a proverb. Education will not; the world is full of educated derelicts. Persistence and determination alone are omnipotent.
**- Calvin Coolidge**

# Chapter 18

## Don't stop after a victory

Satisfaction lies in the effort, not in the attainment.
Full effort is full victory.
- **Albert Einstein**

Most people are always looking for endings. But winners, as they get close to an ending, know they've got to have a new beginning. You've got to have new beginnings all the time.

Most women are taught as they're being brought up, find a prince and live happily ever after. What do you mean live happily ever after? You know it's sad, but the average American couple gets married young, they fight real hard, they save their bucks, they get a down payment on their dream home, they go out and buy new furniture, they get a couple cars, and by the time they're somewhere between 25 and 30 years of age, they have as many material things as their folks do. They are moving ahead unbelievably. And then from there on in they try to maintain it. And from there on in life it gets awful tough because they're trying to maintain. If they were going for more they'd have no problem maintaining. But because their goal is to maintain, many times they lose what they have. If they kept the

> The first step toward going somewhere significant is to decide that you are not going to stay where you are.

same goal orientation they had to get that stuff so much earlier than their parents got it, then holding on to it would have been nothing.

"There are two kinds of men who never amount to very much," Cyrus H.K. Curtis remarked one day to his associate, Edward Bok. "And what kinds are those?" inquired Bok. "Those who cannot do what they are told," replied the famous publisher, "and those who can do nothing else" (Sunday School Journal). Your name is "Stretch" or "Shrink." What's your name? What's your nickname? What are you going to continue to be? "Stretch!" Otherwise you shrink.

The first step toward going somewhere significant is to decide that you are not going to stay where you are. Once you're moving you can keep moving. Does Michael Jordan stop shooting after making his first basket? Did John Grisham quit writing after his first best-seller? Successful people know that each victory buys an admission ticket to a more challenging opportunity.

> **Successful people know that each victory buys an admission ticket to a more challenging opportunity.**

Once you've found a better way, make that better. If you can't think up a new idea, try finding a way to make better use of an old one. All progress is due to those who were not satisfied to let well enough alone. The majority of men meet with failure because of their lack of persistence in creating new plans to add to those that succeed.

"Acorns were good until bread was found" (Francis Bacon). "Where we cannot invent, we may at least improve"

(Charles Caleb Colton). "The important thing is this: to be able at any moment to sacrifice what we are, for what we could become" (Duboise). If at first you do succeed try something harder. "The difference between ordinary and extraordinary is that little extra" (Zig Ziglar).

> **The exciting aspect of enjoying life is really living it to the most, letting it stretch you as far as you can go and then a little further.**

We can all experience success, but how much success do you want? How much do you want?

See, along the line in life, we don't know what's in us until we push ourselves. The ones that know it all don't grow at all. You're there to grow. Life is about growing.

Remember this your lifetime through-
Tomorrow, there will be more to do
And failure waits for all those who stay
With some success made yesterday.
**– Anonymous**

Now, see what you need is to find somebody who encourages you, not discourages you; somebody who believes you can be somebody, be something...and then when you get there encourages you to get a new goal.

People ask us all the time, "Don't you have all you need?" Life's not about your needs. It's about making newer needs, taking wishes and wants and making them needs. The exciting aspect of enjoying life is really living it to the most, letting it stretch you as far as you can go and then a little further.

Whatever your dream is today, in order to keep it vibrant and exciting, you've got to keep extending, expanding and stretching your dreams. It's not getting your dreams that counts. It's chasing them, always chasing them. You know, if you catch them, you've got to have new ones. So you've always got to be working on bigger and better dreams.

**The secret of youth is being busy and having a new growing dream.**

We've got to learn to do those little things that others don't do. I'm setting up as many things to force me to move on as I possibly can. A lot of people settle for things. They become complacent. They develop status. Status is the worst financial-deadening disease in the world. I believe status is bad and has nothing to do with God's way for our life. Status leads to pride and pride "comes before a fall." When you get status you're ready to tumble. You get too proud to do what it takes and too proud to move on.

I remember the first time I lost my dream. And I remember the second time I almost lost my dream. I understand the importance of having a constant dream and a dream ready to follow the next dream.

We've got to have bigger dreams that drive us harder. And every time that you get comfortable, you're in trouble. You'd better get a bigger dream or you're dead. I'm not going to ever have all I need. I'm going to keep needing more. Every time I get more I'm going to need more. Because there's people out here that you and I need to talk to. And we need to help them regardless of our lifestyle.

The saddest feeling in life and what ages you fast is when you're not accomplishing something. You're feeling that guilt and carrying it all the time. The secret of youth is being busy and having a new growing dream. You've got to have a dream and then a new dream. I don't care if you're seventy or seventeen. You've got breath left in you, live it for all it is. Give it all you've got.

You know when fighting begins? When people are no longer productive. When you stop producing, conflict is close behind. You start going out and saying you're worried about how much money a guy is making or wondering if this guy is doing this or doing that, instead of getting your own project going. And you know, it doesn't make any difference where you are financially right now as long as you know where you're going. That's all that counts, knowing where you're going.

I never look for endings, I look for new beginnings. New beginnings. If the project is winding up Sunday night, start something bigger Monday

> **I understand the importance of having a constant dream and a dream ready to follow the next dream.**

morning. We've always got to shoot for new higher, bigger, gigantic goals. By shooting big, even our accidents and our failures don't keep us away from unbelievable success.

To be victorious, and rest on your laurels, that is defeat; to be defeated, and not give up, that is victory.
**– Jozef Pilsudski**

I think there is a world market for about five computers.
**- Thomas J. Watson, IBM, 1943**

With over 15 types of foreign cars already on sale here, the Japanese auto industry isn't likely to carve out a big share of the market for itself.
**- Business Week, 1969**

There is no reason for any individual to have a computer in his home.
**- Kenneth Olson, Digital Equipment, 1977**


Radio has no future. Heavier-than-air flying machines are impossible.
X-rays will prove to be a hoax. I have not the smallest molecule of faith
in aerial navigation other than ballooning.
**- William Thomson, Lord Kelvin (1824-1907)**
**English scientist, president of the Royal Society**


While theoretically and technically television may be feasible, commercially
and financially I consider it an impossibility, a development of which
we need waste little time dreaming.
**- Lee DeForest (1873-1961) American inventor**


The (flying) machines will eventually be fast; they will be used in sport,
but they should not be thought of as commercial carriers.
**- Octave Chanute (1832-1910) French aviation pioneer**


As far as sinking a ship with a bomb is concerned, it just can't be done.
**- Clark Woodward (1877-1967) rear admiral, U.S. Navy**


Who would want to hear actors talk?
**- Harry M. Warner (1881-1958) founder, Warner Bros. Studio**
**(in 1927, considering the possibility of talking pictures)**


Man will never reach the moon regardless of all future scientific advances.
**- Dr. Lee de Forest, inventor of the vacuum tube and father of television**


The telephone is such a flawed communcation device,
we see no use for it in our industry.
**- In a memo to all Western Union offices, 1876**


Anything that can be invented has been invented.
**- Charles H. Duell, Commissioner of the U.S. Patent Office, 1899**


We don't like their sound, and guitar music is on the way out.
**- Decca Recording Company spokesperson when he rejected the Beatles, 1962**

# Chapter 19

## Become the king of your castle

*The most important thing a father can do for his children is to love their mother.* - **Theodore M. Hesburgh**

One of the biggest areas that affects the pursuit of your dreams is in your home. Your spouse and children can be an enormous benefit or an incredible liability. I thank God for Birdie and my children. I never could have done it without them and I can't keep doing it without them.

I've got a teenage girl that I've got a really bad crush on that I've been chasing for almost 50 years. You know? I keep trying to win her. I understand those love songs, I understand you never quit, and you never give up on your goals. I hope you girls understand that for us men, we don't really become a man until we have a woman to be a man for. We must have something or someone to fight for and who is worth fighting for, and you women need to be that someone for us. Because of rejection, one of the hardest things for most men to learn is to compliment a woman. And gals, when your guy compliments, don't argue with him because you know what? If he's in love with you, you are the world's most gorgeous woman. Don't tell him all your bad points. He doesn't see it that way. You're his first-class girl and that's something that's very, very important.

I always laugh when guys have problems with their wives or wives have problems with their husbands, so they think they'll look to new territory for new opportunity. I always think that if you cannot handle what you got, then what makes you think that you can handle another challenge? Take on what you already have and become an expert. Accept her, listen to her, love her, encourage her, and you will earn the right to lead her.

Guys, I'm going to tell you something. We can be as macho as we want, but if you don't learn to love your wife, then you'll never have a reason for your daughters to love you. And if you can't look over and tell your wife, "Hey baby, you're cute, you're wonderful, you're beautiful, you're special," how are you going to tell your daughter that? How's she going to know how to pick a man? For you guys that really don't think your wife is what she should be, then that's partly your fault because you haven't taken time to counsel and to lead her. I want to tell you girls something. It's a man's responsibility to counsel his wife. It's not a wife's job to counsel her husband. It's a wife's job to love and accept her husband. If she can lovingly give him advice, great.

> **We can be as macho as we want, but if you don't learn to love your wife, then you'll never have a reason for your daughters to love you.**

Let me talk for a minute about kids. How do you want your kids to be? Do you want them to be better? Most of us want our kids to be better than us. Well you've got to give them a better start than what you had. The start is not giving them something for nothing. That gives them a worse start. The first thing the kids have to understand is what goals are, how to set them, and how to get them. If the kid's goal is to have a car, and you go out and buy it for him, then you took his goal away. If he didn't work for it, he isn't going to appreciate it. This is about leadership. This is about you winning and being the head of your house, the example for your kids. We cannot count on somebody else to be our kids' hero because they may pick the wrong one. Our job as dads is to be the hero and the example, period. We'll like ourselves better because of it.

Life is fun if you don't get too hung up about it. Have some fun with your wife. Do you guys know how to keep your wife happy? Make her laugh. Take her on dates. Don't make it like something you have to do. The more you lighten up the more you get done.

My dad told me the night before I got married, "Dexter, if it doesn't work you cannot come home, but Birdie can." He was nicely saying that I had accepted a responsibility and he didn't want to hear anything about quitting.

By the way, periodically I'll get somebody to complain to me about their parents. I don't take complaints about parents.

My job is not to create division, only unity. My role is to defend those that are absent. Women rule the world. When the girl's on my side, I just increase my odds by about 80 percent for having great success. You girls don't understand how much control you have over us men. We can play all the macho role we want but you're the ones that can make us cry and make us hurt. We want to be your hero. We want you to admire us. Girls, just practice this over the next couple of weeks. Tell your husband he's a hunk. Tell him he's good-looking and has a good body. Tell him he's your dreamboat. Tell him all that you like about him. Girls, let me tell you. You take care of that man, and he'll kill for you. Women let your man lead. Encourage him but don't correct, criticize, or condemn him. To be the Queen, you have to have a King.

So who can make you feel the greatest? Your own mate. Who can make you feel the worst? Your own mate. Who could confuse you the most? Your own mate. So think before you speak.

It took me a long time to realize I couldn't train Birdie to be me because God didn't give her the job to be me. God gave her the job to be the opposite.

The way you build other people's confidence in themselves is giving them compliments. Edify each other. When Birdie and I sit down to talk to people, they know we're in love. We don't have to tell them. Most people don't have a good marriage. They want a good marriage. They want to be around somebody that's succeeding. So be the example. If you're going to have a relationship in life, one that counts, find the best in others.

You know how you empower kids? Every time you see them doing something good say, "Boy, I'm proud of you for that." All these parents are trying to empower their kids. "My kid's an 'A' student on H.J. Highway High School." They're advertising to everybody else that he's an honor kid. He's an honor kid, but what's he learning? If it's bad stuff, it's not empowering him. It's not what the teacher gives him as a grade; it's how mom and dad give him love.

The biggest rewards you're going to have with your kids is by them seeing mom and dad perform and learning to do the uncommon thing because it was common in their home. Learn to say the most meaningful words ever assembled, "I love you," especially to your wife and your kids.

Each one of us is not complete. God gave you half and your spouse the other half. Your job for life is to make a team made up of two halves. This is my secret. When you get married, pick a mate that has good thinking and that truly loves you. Raise your kids right. Be a great parent. Become responsible, set an example, do what is right—not what feels comfortable. Become one fantastic team and go forward together. Your future is unlimited.

Some pray to marry the person they love, my prayer will somewhat vary;
I humbly pray to Heaven above that I love the person I marry.
**– Rose Pastor Stokes**

To have success but no one to share it with is not success.
**– Dexter Yager**

# Chapter 20

## Success is chasing a dream

*It's not just getting your dreams that counts. It's the chase...
the pursuit that makes life worth living.*
**- Dexter Yager**

Success is the progressive realization of a lifetime dream; it will take your lifetime because it's got to grow and you've got to grow. One of the amazing facts is that if you pursue your dream diligently enough, the dream begins to pursue you also.

So many times, happiness is a matter of what you're concentrating on. You can try and concentrate on your problems and your pain, or you can concentrate on your dreams. Too many people concentrate on their problems and not enough on their dreams. Happiness is not getting your dreams. Happiness is chasing your dreams. And in one of the most important papers that this country is built on, we are guaranteed the pursuit of happiness. Isn't that right?

Our founding fathers knew what success was. They understood the pursuit of happiness. In other words, they were all very successful men who signed the Declaration of Independence, the Constitution, those papers that this country was founded and built on. They understood things that a lot of so-called educated, smart people today don't understand. One of them is that happiness only remains happiness when you're pursuing it. Getting something is just accomplishing what you knew you were going to do. Now you've got to start going after what else you know you've got to do.

I remember when I was in high school, one of my buddies, Rich Bilby, worked on his dad's farm. We'd go to the store, and he'd buy everybody a Coke. I said, "someday, I'll be able to pick up the bill for everybody." So many times, we go out and Birdie laughs because I'm trying to grab the bill all the time. It's something I wanted to be able to do, pick up the tab. Not having to reach in my wallet and figure out what I could afford to eat. Not worrying about what it costs.

Freedom. What level of freedom do you want? How high do you want to fly? How big is your dream going to be? Are you going to allow somebody to talk you out of it, or are you just going to dig in deeper? If we don't make it this year, we don't stop—we just reset the goal. You set a vision so far beyond where you can hardly even comprehend, that it will seem like a fantasy, but you're committed to it. You don't set easy goals; right goals are there to stretch you.

> **It's not just getting your dreams that counts. It's the chase...the pursuit.**

Whatever your dream is, to stay vibrant and exciting, you've got to keep extending, expanding and stretching your dreams. It's not just getting your dreams that counts. It's the chase...the pursuit. Will you go share it with somebody else?

Don't go from a dream program to a maintenance program. You don't maintain what you have, really. When you stop dreaming you start falling. The power of life, the energy, is in your dreams. It's not in your I.Q. A bigger dream will give you a bigger I.Q. A bigger dream will let you handle the major challenges of life.

Ben Franklin said the average American dies at twenty-one and is buried at sixty-five. People say, "Well how come some people don't make it big?" Their thinking stops them. It "dies." Any time you get in your comfort zone you are in trouble. One thing I've learned is don't get in a comfort zone. Stay in a dream zone.

---

## When you stop dreaming you start falling.

---

I used to have a Comfort Zone, where I knew I couldn't fail.
The same four walls of busy work, were really more like jail.
I longed so much to do the things I'd never done before,
but I stayed inside my Comfort Zone, and paced the same old floor.
I said it didn't matter, that I wasn't doing much.
I said I didn't care for things, like dreams, goals and such.
I claimed to be so busy, with the things inside my zone,
but deep inside I longed for, something special of my own.
I couldn't let my life go by, just watching others win.
I held my breath and stepped outside and let the change begin.
I took a step and with new strength I'd never felt before,
I kissed my Comfort Zone "goodbye" and closed and locked the door.
If you are in a Comfort Zone, afraid to venture out,
remember that all winners were at one time filled with doubt.
A step of faith and the Word of God, can make your dreams come true.
Greet your future with a smile, Success is there for you!
**- Anonymous**

# Chapter 20

At the end of every day of every year, two things must remain unshakable: our constancy of purpose and our continuous discontent with the present.

**- Robert Goizieta, Coca-Cola**

Happiness...is not a destination: it is a manner of traveling. Happiness is not an end in itself. It is a by-product of working, playing, loving, and living.

**- Haim Ginott**

# Chapter 21

## Success is a decision

If you don't run your own life, someone else will.
- John Atkinson

Decisions are what transform an idea into a reality. Your destiny is not a matter of chance; it is a matter of choice. Many people have the right aims in life—they just never get around to pulling the trigger.

Indecision will paralyze the flow of your faith, for faith demands a decision before it can work. Like all parts of your life, your beliefs and your success are a decision.

> **The more somebody does for you, (that you've not earned through performance), the weaker you are.**

Every accomplishment, great or small, starts with the decision. Not everything that is met can be changed, but nothing can be changed until it is met.

The Bible says that a double-minded man is unstable in all his ways. I know people who are triple and quadruple-minded. I can't imagine what kind of trouble they're in! It's not the difference between people that's the difficulty. It's the indifference.

The more you take responsibility away from people, the more they expect from you and the less they get to be on their own. The more somebody does for you, (that you've not earned through performance), the weaker you are. You can't increase while letting others make decisions for you.

People who demand neutrality in any situation are not really neutral, but in favor of things not changing. "Mistrust the man who finds everything good, the man who finds everything evil and still more the man who is indifferent to everything." says Larry Bielat.

There is one guaranteed way to not grow, and that is to be indecisive. Meet the little problems and opportunities of your life with a decision. The most unhappy people we know are those who can never make a decision. An indecisive man can never be said to belong to himself. Don't worry about not making a decision; someone will make it for you. An indecisive person is like a blind man looking in a dark room for a black cat that isn't there.

**Be decisive even if it means you'll sometimes be wrong.**

I don't care if you choose not to reach your dreams; that's your choice. What would bother me is if you blamed not making it on somebody else. We can blame all we want, but that's a kid's way, and you're an adult. Others can help you, but ultimately you've got to make the decision.

A man with one watch knows what time it is; a man with two is never quite sure. Until you are decisively committed, there is hesitancy and the temptation to draw back, followed by ineffectiveness. Listen to what you say. If you hear yourself saying, "I've decided," you're on the path towards an exciting and productive life. As soon as you decide to do something with your life, your life will change.

Success is a decision not an accident. The Bible tells us we're to be *in* the world but not *of* it because the world will tell you all the wrong answers. Success is a decision, one that you make today.

The signers of the Declaration of Independence had in mind for each one of us the freedom to choose, to work, to dream, and the freedom to pursue whatever it is we want.

*"We hold these truths to be self-evident, that all men are created equal, that they are endowed by their creator with certain unalienable rights, that among these are life, liberty, and the pursuit of happiness."*

**A man with one watch knows what time it is; a man with two is never quite sure.**

What that passage from the Declaration says to me is that all of us were created equal, with the right to become unequal if we choose to. Each and every one of us chooses our own life. What are you choosing for you, your wife, your kids, and your future? We choose our life. What are you choosing for you, your wife, your kids, and your future? I'll tell you the day I had that stroke at forty-six years old that it might've been it forever. If I'd had a job, I'd have been fired. The right side of my body still isn't working perfectly. There are still lots of things I can't do, but I can still build my business and pursue my dreams. It doesn't stop me. People see us the way they think we are. But more important than that is the way you see yourself and the way you think you are.

You're going to run across people who are going to tell you about where you didn't succeed. Success is never easy, but it's easier than failure—you've got to live with that all your life. Success always follows a decision.

Too many people spend too much of their time worrying about what somebody else thinks, and they don't end up where they ought to be. If you're going to succeed, you've got to know where you're going. You've got to make up your mind what you want. You cannot stay in neutral. I'll put it this way, "Your least favorite color should be beige."

Based on the decisions we make, there are really only two kinds of people: those who are willing to take the responsibility and do whatever it takes to make something happen, and those who are willing to take whatever they can. The givers and the takers. The givers always end up on top because God's got a rule, and you cannot outgive God. God's rule is *the more you give the more you're going to get. The more that you take, the more you're going to lose.* The most important thing that we've got going is our willingness to dream and to not let anybody steal it. When your dream's gone, you're dead. That's life, that's hope, that's everything.

> **God's rule is the more you give the more you're going to get. The more that you take, the more you're going to lose.**

Be decisive, even if it means you'll sometimes be wrong. A key to your future is that you can still choose, you can still decide. What you commit yourself to be will change you from what you are into what you can be. Decision determines destiny.

The refusal to choose is a form of choice; disbelief is a form of belief.
**- Frank Barron**

Once you make a decision, the universe conspires to make it happen.
**- Ralph Waldo Emerson**

# Chapter 22

## Success is hard work

The best way to raise your self-image
is by doing what you know needs to be done.
**- Dexter Yager**

Ideas are funny things; they do not work unless you do. Promotion is achieved by motion. No rule of success will work if you don't. Do you have time to kill? How about working it to death? "Beware of the man who does not translate his words into deeds" (Theodore Roosevelt). Knowing without doing is like plowing without sowing. Ambition never gets anywhere until it forms a partnership with work.

So many people quit who were so much better than me. They were "want-to-be's," but not "work-a-be's." Few dreams come true by themselves. The test of a person lies in action. I have never heard of anyone stumbling onto something big

**The smallest deed done is better than the greatest intention.**

while sitting down. Even a mosquito doesn't get a slap on the back until he starts to work. A famous poem by an unknown author states, "Sitting still and wishing makes no person great, the good Lord sends the fishing, but you must dig the bait." The smallest deed done is better than the greatest intention. History is made whenever you take the right action. Action is the proper fruit of knowledge. Getting an idea should be like sitting on a tack; it should make you jump up and do something.

"Go to the ant, thou sluggard; consider her ways, and be wise: which having no guide, overseer, or ruler, provideth her meat in the summer, and gathereth her food in the harvest" (Proverbs 6:6-8). Nothing preaches better than this ant, yet she says nothing. You earn respect only by action; inaction earns disrespect.

Some people find life an empty dream because they put nothing into it. Every time one man expresses an idea, he finds ten men who thought of it before—but they only thought. Mark Twain said, "Thunder is good, thunder is impressive, but it is lightning that does the work." The test of this book is that the reader goes away not saying, "What an interesting book" but, "I will do something!"

You've got the greatest opportunity to follow your dreams, but you've got to work. And I'll tell you something. Anybody who tells you you don't have to work for success is lying to you. Things don't just happen; you make them happen. I work hard, and I love my work.

> **Anybody who tells you you don't have to work for success is lying to you.**

You don't run from a fight because the bully will chase you. Anybody who grew up had some bullies. Right, guys? We don't go looking for a fight. We're glad if we go two, three years without one. You can only go so long before somebody bullies you. And you're going to be put in that corner. You've got to make a decision, and the moment you run, you'll be chased all your life.

Climb out of the grandstand and onto the playing field. You can't fulfill your destiny on a theory...it takes WORK.

None of the secrets of success will work unless you do. You are made for action. Success simply takes good ideas and puts them to work.

Prosperity is something God gives to his people after they work, stretch, survive, and become strong enough to be worthy of it. It's not just a matter of whether you love God or you worship God. Remember, He said, "Faith without work is dead." It's a matter of whether you have done something and served Him enough to be able to be

> I will tell you one thing for sure. If you're not succeeding as much as you want, then you've got to learn to work harder, and then learn to work smarter.

in a position of authority. That's why you've got to get down and scratch around with the chickens so you're worthy to fly with the eagles. Look through the Bible. Tell me who had the easy road.

I will tell you one thing for sure: If you're not succeeding as much as you want, then you've got to learn to work harder, and then learn to work smarter. And if you haven't worked harder, then you cannot learn how to work smarter because it takes failing enough times to go out and say, "I've got to fix this so I don't fail as much." If you want more, get better. The only way you can get better is change your head. And when you change your head, the money comes later. You're making an investment in yourself.

You want a little business; treat it like a little business. Spend a little bit of time. Invest a little bit of money. But if you want a big business, then treat it like a big business. Invest a lot of time, work hard and put the money in it, then you'll have a big business.

"Striving for success without hard work is like trying to harvest where

**If you want more, get better.**

you haven't planted" (David Bly). What you believe doesn't amount to very much unless it causes you to wake up from your dream and start working. You cannot just dream yourself into what you could be. The only time a lazy person ever succeeds is when he tries to do nothing. A famous old saying says it best: "Laziness travels so slowly, poverty soon overtakes it."

When you are lazy, you must work twice as hard. It is a trying time for the person who is always trying to get something for nothing. Some say nothing is impossible, yet there are a lot of people doing nothing every day.

If you ever look around, you'll hear many people tell you you're working too hard. You're too involved. You're too committed. Now I ask all of us, when are we going to slow down, when are we going to be tired? All we have to do is look at the losers and know we don't want to. We don't want to be where they're at financially, physically, or mentally. I've had younger people tell me they wouldn't want to do what I'm doing because they just want the rewards. You couldn't enjoy the rewards if you weren't doing the work; otherwise, it's a highly paid welfare trip. But when you do the work, you deserve the rewards.

Many years ago, I was at the White House and Ronald Reagan mentioned something—a special invitation at the White House. We got a nice, engraved little card. The President and his wife wanted us there at 5:00 p.m., and we were there at 5:00

p.m. I think he made such a great statement. He said, "I'm accused always of supporting the rich, but I don't." He said, "I'm just trying to leave the door of opportunity open so the future people of America still can have the dream and become rich."

**You set your goals and then work like it's impossible to fail.**

Don't tell me that you've got a lack of self-confidence and what you cannot do. You haven't tried to do it yet. You try to do it, and you'll find out eventually that you're one of the best. You know how you get to be the best in anything? Make up your mind that you're going to be the best. Work at it, play at it, enjoy it, and make a commitment to it.

You set your goals and then work like it's impossible to fail. You hear that? Don't work like it's impossible to succeed. Work like it's impossible to fail. Your destiny is your choice. We can't control everything, but we can control our activity which controls our results. So you go for the big picture. Work like it's impossible to fail and you'll succeed beyond anybody's belief. Don't put limitations on your dreams and on your future.

If you want your kids to be proud of you, go out and perform. Performance is the answer. You've got to perform to be somebody in life, and the most important person

**If you want your kids to be proud of you, go out and perform.**

that you've got to become is you. I don't care what anybody else thinks of me. I'll love them in spite of their stupidity. The important thing is that I'm a winner, and I know it. The important thing is that you are a winner, but do you know it? If you know it, you're going to live on it, and you're going to perform.

When you learn to respect people, the doors will open up so that you can become friends with those people. Hey, I've known the last five presidents of the United States personally. Not bad for a little kid from Rome, New York, that hasn't got great English and barely got through high school. Performance is what makes the difference.

Man, when you work you feel good. When you're doing nothing, you don't feel good. I'm a man who will go out and perform in spite of whatever obstacles life has put in front of me. I'm not going to complain. I will still be a man worthy of being married to. I'm not about to sit around and cry the blues and have a pretty young wife who wonders why she married me. I will go perform and get the goodies for that gal. She was worth getting the goodies for and she's special. And you know, I believed that when I was dating her, and I believed that when I married her.

Keep in mind the words of Hamilton Holt: "Nothing worthwhile comes easily. Half effort does not produce half results. It produces no results. Work, continuous work and hard work is the only way to accomplish results that last."

The only place where success comes before work is the dictionary.
**– Arthur Brisbane**

Opportunity usually shows up disguised in overalls.
**– Anonymous**

I have found that success is measured not so much by the position attained in life as by the obstacles which have been overcome in attaining that position.
**– Dr. Booker T. Washington**

The best prize life offers is the chance to work hard at work worth doing.
**– Anonymous**

# Chapter 23

## Success is all about failure

*I am the biggest failure in my industry
and that is why I am the biggest success.*
**- Dexter Yager**

Mistakes have hidden powers to help us, but they fail in that mission when we blame other people for our mistakes. When you use excuses, you give up your power to change and improve. "Never mind whom you praise, but be careful whom you blame" (Edmond Gosse).

> **Success is not what people think it is. Success is all about failure.**

We all experience failure and make mistakes. In fact, successful people always have more failure in their lives than average people. Great people throughout history have all failed at some point in their lives. Those who do not expect anything are never disappointed; those who never try never fail. Anyone who is currently achieving anything in life is simultaneously risking failure. It is always better to fail in doing something than to excel at doing nothing. A flawed diamond is more valuable than a perfect brick. People who have no failures have few victories.

Success is not what people think it is. Success is all about failure. The person who fails the most, normally succeeds at the highest level.

I've done stupid things. I was thinking of some of the many stupid things I've done. I remember sitting up here on a podium and tapping this girl named Nancy on the leg. We were sitting there and I'm saying, "This is the year, girl." I didn't stop to think that it was Nancy Reagan's leg I was tapping. Talk about a mistake! It was the year her husband became president of the United States. I'll never forget how Mr. Reagan and I got on our hands and knees with another guy and prayed that he'd be president of the United States. There's power in prayer.

Birdie and I probably have been about as dumb as we could ever be in everything that we've ever done. But at the same time, we always wanted to make everything we ever did work. We both have a little stubborn streak in us that is tough to deal with. When you're stubborn enough, you cannot tolerate failure. If you want success you have to learn that you're going to deal with failure. Failure prepares you for handling success.

**A winner takes a problem and converts it into a solution. He takes a tragedy and creates a blessing out of it.**

I step out on faith every day. Sometimes it's right and sometimes it's wrong. But I'd rather be wrong than miss the opportunity to change something.

The saying that you cannot teach old dogs new tricks is a lie because we can do whatever we feel that we need to do. We either have to make the right choice or the wrong choice. We can stay stuck in our mistakes, or we can admit the wrong choice and get up and go on with our lives.

Success consists of getting up just one more time than you fall. "You don't drown by falling in the water, you drown by staying there," said author Ed Cole. Proverbs 28:13 (TLB) says, "A man who refuses to admit his mistakes can never be successful, but if he confesses and forsakes them, he gets another chance."

If you have a dream without problems, you don't really have a legitimate dream. Have the attitude of Louisa May Alcott: "I am not afraid of storms, for I am learning how to sail my ship." Samuel Lover said, "Circumstances are the rulers of the weak; but they are the instruments of the wise." Don't let your problems take the lead. You take the lead. The problem you face is simply an opportunity for you to do your best.

While you're failing, don't focus on the failure; focus on the dream and the reward. The hardest thing for people to understand in success is learning how to maximize their failures. It's not the failures that destroy you. It's how you handle them. We all tell the story about Edison discovering more than a thousand different ways the light bulb didn't work. Are you going to find more than a thousand ways that it doesn't work, or are you going to make it work? That's what success is all about, having more failures than successes. While everybody's keeping track of your successes and failures, you're following your dreams. Don't let your failures of the past become the failures of the future.

It's not a problem to have to start over again. The blessing is that I'm alive to start. You've got to look at things in the right perspective. Sure, I had this stroke. I'm not as well off in some ways as I was, but I'm more appreciative of what

I've got. I count my blessings all the time. Get your faith in the positive, not in the negative.

A winner always takes a problem and converts it to a solution. He takes a tragedy and creates a blessing out of it. God wants us to be blessed, but will we allow Him to help us?

It doesn't make any difference when you get knocked down if you don't stay down for the count. No winner ever stays down. It's not how far you fall but how high you bounce that makes all of the difference. Get yourself back up and start fighting again. The fact that you won the fight once doesn't make any difference. I want to fight until the day after they nail the top on the coffin, then I may say, "Hey, I guess we hang it up here and move on to heaven and start working up there because we've got a job to do."

I want you to take home a dream from this book. I don't care what the dream is and what mistakes you've made. The death of your dream will not happen because of a failure. Its death will come from indifference and apathy.

> No winner ever stays down.

I'm committed to live my life every day by getting up every morning and counting my blessings. I'm committed to get out of bed, even though I have physical pain and thank God for that hurt because if I wasn't hurting, I'd be dead. I thank God for those problems because they're blessings to me.

So many people get bitter. You cannot get bitter, you've got to get better. Look to work better. Look to dream better. Every time we have an experience we get a valuable education. Why should we be smart and broke?

More people get hung up on the bad stuff rather than the

good stuff, and that's why they end up broke instead of rich. If we're going to become rich we've got to keep our thinking straight. We've got to start developing success habits. We've got to quit taking things personally. There's only one God that ever walked on this earth who was perfect, and he was crucified. So don't expect perfection in yourself. If you do, you're going to get hung.

The key is that when you succeed, know you can do it again. But when you keep failing, you think that you're going to keep repeating it. You're going to keep believing in what you do, and you've got to get a couple successes under your belt to know that you can do it again. I've done it once; I can do it a hundred times.

It's awfully hard when someone who is interviewing you tries to call your success luck. That's the biggest insult that you can give to anybody. I don't care what you've done with your life, you've made some decisions and that wasn't an accident. We might have been blessed, but everybody in the world has some kind of a blessing. There are so many people who are always counting what they consider their tragedies instead of their blessings. Out of every tragedy in each of our lives come blessings.

> More people get hung up on the bad stuff rather than the good stuff, and that's why they end up broke instead of rich.

It is better to fail in doing something than to excel in doing nothing. Mistakes and failure are two of the surest stepping stones to success. "Most people think of success and failure as opposites, but they are actually both products of the same process" (Roger Von Oech). Your season of failure is the best time for sowing your seeds of success.

Every now and then, people come up and they'll say, "Well, this isn't fair." I remember Jerry Meadows saying, "Whoever told you life was fair?" Each one of us has a different cross to bear, and you've got to learn to like your cross. There's an old saying—"If everybody had to bring their cross, put it up in a pile, and look at what's there, most of them would take their cross home with them." They'd find out whatever they think is so bad is not as bad compared to what other people have to bear. Another old saying is true, "Everybody is about as happy as they make up their mind to be or about as miserable as they choose to be."

I've had people say, "Oh yeah, as successful as you are, I can see why you're happy and why you have a good attitude." I say, "No, no, no you've got it backwards. I'm as successful as I am and I'm as happy as I am because I had that attitude years ago when I was broke. With everything that happened, I tried to see the sunny side of it." You cannot think that the world's out to get you. You've got to say, "This is my world, and I'm going to get it regardless of how much it fights."

> A lot of people have a poor self image in life because they're reading the score that other people are keeping on them.

The road to success is always under construction. Do you know why it's under construction? It's being worked on because it's traveled on and detoured on so much. Some people go out there and mess the road up so they can go home. But a real committed person understands the dips and bumps of a much-traveled road. They understand that it gets smoother at the top because fewer people travel that road. But so many people get discouraged at the beginning when they hit the ruts, dips, and bumps.

You've got to be like a farmer. The farmer plants his crop year after year, knowing he's going to survive. Sure, one year the cold wipes out his crop, and another year the wind wipes it out. But he knows he's going to have some crop left. He keeps planting because he knows that every time he has a crop he's got to save some of that seed to replant it. If he keeps planting, it's going to multiply. He's got to harvest. What you sow, so shall you reap. We've got to learn to sow a lot. Not everything that we sow is going to make it. The wind and the sun are going to dry some out. All kinds of circumstances are going to happen. In spite of all of that, we hold on to the scripture that says, "Don't be weary in well doing, for in due season we shall reap a harvest if we don't give up."

It's not the score that somebody else keeps on your life; it's the score you keep. It makes a difference. A lot of people have a poor self image in life because they're reading the score that other people are keeping on them. You've got to start scoring every time you win. Remember your wins not your losses. Nobody wins every time, but if you only count all your losses, then you'll think you've lost every time. The man who believes he can do something is probably right. And so is the man who believes that he cannot. Winners expect to win in advance.

# Chapter 23

The greatest mistake you can make in life is to continually fear that you will make one. "Don't be afraid to fail. Don't waste energy trying to cover up failure. If you're not failing, you're not growing," says H. Stanley Judd.

The men who try to do something and fail are infinitely better than those who try to do nothing and succeed.
**- Lloyd Jones**

Learn from your mistakes: failure is the opportunity to begin again more intelligently.
**- Henry Ford**

If your life is free of failure, maybe you are not taking enough risk.
**- Anonymous**

Many of life's failures are people who did not realize how close they were to success when they gave up. I never experienced failure. I only found 9,999 ways the light bulb wouldn't work before finding a way it would.
**- Thomas Edison**

There is a sure way to avoid criticism: be nothing and do nothing. Kill off all ambition. The remedy never fails. Do what you feel in your heart is right— for you'll be criticized anyway. You'll be damned if you do, and damned if you don't
**- Eleanor Roosevelt**

One of the great examples of successfully handling adversity can be found in Abraham Lincoln. Consider his record:

| | | | |
|---|---|---|---|
| Failed in business | 1831 | Defeated for Congress | 1843 |
| Defeated for Legislature | 1832 | Defeated for Senate | 1855 |
| Failed in business again | 1833 | Defeated for Vice President | 1856 |
| Sweetheart died | 1835 | Defeated for Senate | 1858 |
| Suffered Nervous Breakdown | 1836 | Elected President | 1860 |

# Chapter 24

## Success is being in pursuit of excellence

*The pursuit of excellence is gratifying and healthy.*
*The pursuit of perfection is frustrating, neurotic, and a terrible waste of time.*
**- Edwin Bliss**

A while back, I got my foot fixed by a prominent doctor who was committed to doing it right even though his office was damaged. He said "Excuse my office, Dexter. I know it's the first time you've ever been here, and it's a mess. The insurance company wanted me to close down because two weeks ago we had a fire next door, and it burned everything out." He was in a big shopping center, and they wanted him to close down. He told them that he couldn't afford to close down, even though they agreed to pay him two to three thousand dollars a day for a month to be out of business. He said that in a month he would lose a lot of the flow of his patients. They would start going someplace else. He said, "So against their advice, I've gone ahead and gone out and gotten new equipment and everything else and I'm operating. My practice is more important than a few dollars from the insurance company. So we've got a lot of little things you're going to have to deal with, so don't judge my practice on today. When we get back in full steam, it's going to be different. I know that you're going to get better treatment at my worst than what you're going to get someplace else at their best." I saw right away that leadership's the same in all areas. Excellence matters.

The biggest mistake you can make in life is not to be true to the best you know. George Bernard Shaw remarked, "Keep yourself clean and bright; you are the window through which you must see the world." Follow Ralph Sockman's advice: "Give the best that you have to the highest you know—and do it now."

Character is the real foundation of all worthwhile success. A good question to ask yourself is, "What kind of world would it be if everybody were just like me?"

You won't become good by deciding not to be bad. You won't excel by deciding not to be mediocre. And you won't win by deciding not to lose. You must be for something. I'm for purpose, dreams and excellence. And whether it's our country, whether it's our mate, whether it's our children, whether it's our group or our business, we've got to find the best and focus on the best.

> **Living a double life will get you nowhere twice as fast.**

Living a double life will get you nowhere twice as fast. "Thoughts lead on to purposes; purposes go forth in action; actions form habits; habits decide character; and character fixes our destiny," said Tryon Edwards. Proverbs asserts, "A good name is rather to be chosen great riches." Character is something you either have or are. Don't try to make something for yourself; instead, try to make something of yourself.

Don't just seek success. Instead, seek excellence, and you will find both. Work to become, not to acquire. Do the very best you can, and leave the results to take care of themselves. People are funny; they spend money they don't have, to buy things they don't need, to impress people they don't like. Success is not found in achieving what you aim at but in aiming at what you ought to achieve. "Happy is the man who doesn't give in and do wrong when he is tempted, for afterwards he will get as his reward the crown of life that God has promised those who love Him" (James 1:12, LB).

There is always a heavy demand for fresh mediocrity—don't give in to it. Instead, be easily satisfied with the very best. When you are delivering your very best is when you will feel most successful. "Excellence demands that you be better than yourself" (Ted Engstrom). Never sell your principles for popularity or you'll find yourself bankrupt in the worst way.

> **Don't just seek success. Instead, seek excellence, and you will find both.**

The passengers on a commercial airliner have been seated and are awaiting the cockpit crew to get them under way. A murmur is heard in the back of the plane, and a few passengers on the aisle glance back to see the pilot and copilot, both wearing large, dark sunglasses, making their way up to the cockpit.

However, the pilot is using a white cane, bumping into passengers right and left as he stumbles down the aisle, and the co-pilot is using a seeing-eye guide dog. As they pass by the rows of passengers there are nervous giggles heard, as people are thinking that it must be some sort of practical joke.

But a few minutes after the cockpit door has closed behind them the engines start spooling up and the airplane taxis out to the runway. The passengers look at each other with some uneasiness, whispering among themselves and shifting uneasily or gripping the armrests more tightly. As the airplane starts accelerating rapidly, people begin panicking. Some passengers are praying, and as the plane gets closer and closer to the end of the runway, passengers become more and more hysterical!

Finally, when the airplane has less than a few seconds of runway left, the shouts of horror fill the cabin as everyone screams at once, but at the very last moment the airplane lifts off and is airborne!!!

Up in the cockpit, the co-pilot breathes a sigh of relief and turns to the captain, "You know, one of these days the passengers are going to scream too late, and we're going to get killed!"

Sometimes you can allow compromise to go pretty far without shouting out against it. How far are you willing to go?

I know a couple of guys who are 75 years old and make me look like I've got no muscle on me at all. I keep telling myself when I grow up I'm going to look just like them. How many people 75 years old do you want to look like?

**People are funny; they spend money they don't have, to buy things they don't need, to impress people they don't like.**

It's amazing. After I had my first stroke, they said "Man, you can't protect yourself. You've got a few bucks and somebody could knock you off." The funny thing is that I know if I went out with those two "old" buddies, I know any rough guy would look at the two of them, and he wouldn't mess with me. What do you want to look like? What do you want to be like? God made you to be the best, not to be second class. We've got to grow up and we've got to grow into it. We've got to dream. We've got to believe.

> **Never sell your principles for popularity or you'll find yourself bankrupt in the worst way.**

In the race for excellence there is no finish line.

There is a way to do it better...find it.
**– Thomas Edison**

The door to self-improvement opens from the inside.
**– Anonymous**

The quality of a person's life is in direct proportion to their commitment to excellence, regardless of their chosen field of endeavor.
**– Vince Lombardi**

One of the marks of successful people is that they are action-oriented. One of the marks of average people is that they are talk-oriented.
**– Brian Tracey**

# Chapter 25

## Success is a habit

Motivation is what gets you started.
Habit is what keeps you going.
**- Jim Rohn**

Men and women who succeed create habits, and then the habits create the men and women. Anybody that's highly successful is automatically a creature of pre-decided habits. Birdie and I know where we came from. We know what we've accomplished, and the biggest thing that we have accomplished is not a large business. It's having developed working habits and understanding that if you work hard enough often enough, enough good things will happen that you will pass on to others.

I hear too many people saying things like, "Oh well, I don't like to do that. That makes me embarrassed, or that makes me uncomfortable." Join the crowd. Join the ranks of leaders. Don't think that just because somebody's a leader that they've never been uncomfortable, or that they've never done things that they didn't know how to do. That's ridiculous. In the beginning of this business, everything we did was uncomfortable because we didn't know what we were doing.

You've got to really watch your habits. Your habits make or break you. Every one of you has the potential to be anything you choose but you got to develop the habits, create the attitude, and be the example to others. Somebody asked the other day, "Do you like going to the gym?" "I love it."

"You really like it?"

"I've got to love it for what I'm paying."

I chose to love it. Otherwise, I'm going to die. You understand that? See, people say you cannot love what you do. I chose to love what I do and now it's a good habit for me.

I used to want to guarantee everybody success. If they don't listen, you can't guarantee them anything. Only you can guarantee you anything. How does this happen? By your daily, weekly, monthly and yearly habits. Nobody else can guarantee you anything. You've got to make the commitment. If you want your life to change, you've got to change.

I remember when my dad taught me that plumbers never bite their fingernails. All you've got to do is think...clogged toilet, who fixes it? But you know it's funny, I never had that habit as a kid. But when I got into business and got rolling, guess what? You get a little snag in your fingernail, get to a red light, you're in traffic, and all of the sudden you start biting that nail. You're just trying to smooth it out. Next thing you know, it's down to the quick, and you've bitten all of them.

**Every one of you has the potential to be anything you choose, but you have to develop the habits, create the attitude, and be the example to others.**

I let that happen in the early days of business. I was out doing a meeting one night when a guy came up and said, "You talk like you've got confidence but looking at your nails, you haven't." And I said, "Oh well, that's a little thing. Are you going to get hung up on it? Remember the business plan I shared? It's your opportunity. I'm doing what I want with it. Don't let that hang you up just because I bite my nails." But I went home, and I thought about it. I said, "I've got to quit biting my nails; it costs me money." So I decided I was going to bite my thumbnail only. Within a short period of time, I had nine long nails, and it looked like one was broken. After I had developed the habit, it was no problem to quit biting the thumbnail. You have to learn a success pattern that works.

**If you want your life to change, you've got to change.**

We tell people to watch their words. It's one of the most important habits to really get a handle on because you're snared by the words of your mouth, and we tell people to watch what you say because whatever is inside of you is your outside strength. When you confess failure you possess failure. When you confess success you possess success. You need to learn to get up in the morning with a habit of confessing success.

It's up to you to decide that you're going some place with your life. God didn't make you to be broke. God didn't make you to just survive the rest of your life. God didn't make you so that you have dreams you can't get. Anything the mind can believe and conceive, it can achieve, but first, we've got to believe in it. It doesn't matter how much I believe in you. You've got to believe in you. You've got to believe enough to get yourself up and go do what you need to get done.

Decide to develop habits that force you to be active.

We had to change some habits and do some things we'd never done before. It's uncomfortable when you have to do things that you have never done before. It stretches you and makes you uncomfortable. But, the good news is that when God stretches you, you never come back to your original shape.

Men do not determine their destiny. Men determine their habits and their habits determine their destiny.
**- Mike Murdock**

Your mind will be like its habitual thoughts; for the soul becomes dyed with the color of its thoughts.
**- Marcus Aurelius**

# Chapter 26

## Success is all about relationships

*"Personal relationships are the fertile soil from which all advancement, all success, all achievement in real life grows."*

**- Ben Stein**

Everyone wants to feel like they're somebody. Here is a vital thing to remember: the more valuable and special you make people feel, the more they will respond to you.

> Relationships not only determine your level of achievement—but how much you enjoy the journey.

Human relationships are one of the most important fundamentals, but it's a subject that isn't taught in school. It's not taught at very many places at all, even though it's a skill that's vital for success in anything. Building relationships hasn't always been easy for me. Some people say, "Dexter, you are great at this but that is not my strong point," or "I'm not really good at it," or "I don't really like people." I tell them that the answer is real simple—change. Until you learn how to build relationships, strategy will mean very little. I used to be awful at meeting people. I was nervous. I was a stutterer. I didn't have any confidence. I thought that successful people wouldn't be interested in me or in what I had to say because I hadn't achieved any success yet. I had to change. I changed the way I thought, began building relationships, and now some of my best friends are celebrities and even world leaders. My list of friends has expanded. I've developed a list of fundamentals that I use to build relationships. Take an honest look at yourself as I go through them, because relationships not only determine your level of achievement—but how much you enjoy the journey.

> **Whenever you have a chance to praise someone, don't let it pass you by.**

1.) Speak to people. A simple "hello" or "good morning" as you pass someone lights up the moment and makes the world a friendlier place.

2.) Smile at people. The most powerful thing anyone can do to become instantly attractive is smile. You've heard me say that I don't talk to strangers—I talk to friends I haven't met yet. A smile shows people that you're friendly and you want to develop a friendship.

3.) Call people by their names—and work hard at remembering names. When you remember someone's name, you're giving them a compliment. You're saying, "I think you're important enough to remember."

4.) Be friendly and helpful. Don't ever act like people are a problem. Remember that building a relationship is the goal. People aren't a problem—they're the key.

5.) Be genuinely interested in people. Find out about their lives and what makes them tick, their goals, and their dreams. Focus on what they're interested in, not what you're interested in.

6.) Be generous with praise and cautious with criticism. Most people have a low self-image, even if they don't act like it. You might see someone with all kinds of status. A lot of times, the cars and custom-made clothes are there to hide a poor self-image. That's why it's so powerful to praise everyone. Whenever you have a chance to praise someone, don't let it pass you by and be specific. Whether it's husband-wife relationships, parent-child relationships, or business relationships, compliments are major things. Every day I try to compliment people on all their successes, no matter how small those successes may seem to them. Spend your time developing, not criticizing.

7.) Be considerate of people's feelings. Put yourself in the other guy's shoes. How would you want someone to talk to you?

8.) Learn to give service. What makes us strong and powerful is what we do for others—not what we sit around waiting for them to do for us. Serving other people doesn't make us servants—it fulfills us.

9.) Learn to trust people. Trust is what builds lasting relationships. Don't trust people because they're perfect; you trust them because you love them. It's when somebody knows your weaknesses and trusts you anyway that it means the most. To believe in a person who has failed is love.

> **Take a look at what you're getting back from people, because that's an honest gauge of what you're putting out.**

10.) Have a good sense of humor. I learned to laugh at myself. When you don't take anything too seriously, people feel comfortable around you.

Your rewards are determined by the problems you solve for others. You've got to turn these 10 principles into habits that you do everyday. People will begin to respond more positively to you. It won't be because you know more facts or practice more techniques. It's because you've mastered treating people with respect. That's what people respond to. Take a look at what you're getting back from people, because that's an honest gauge of what you're putting out. Turn these ten principles into habits and you may be surprised at the improvements.

Birdie and I aren't superstars. Everything we have has come about because we've taught other people how to become superstars. It's impossible to truly succeed unless you first help others succeed. My goal has always been to make people feel so special and good about themselves when they are

**No matter what your profession is, success in life is about relationships.**

with me that they can't wait to get back together again. I've never thought of my business relationships as business relationships. Everyone in my business is a friend before a business partner or associate. I've built my entire business around making friends and then making those friends even better friends. The basic building block of my business is friendship. Whenever I autograph things for people one of the messages I write over and over is "you're special," because I honestly believe that everyone is special. When people are special to you, you make it a point to learn the little things about them that make them unique. You learn their personalities, their likes and dislikes, their moods. You learn what motivates them. The more you know about a person, the easier it is to help them become the best they can be. You learn how to communicate with them. You understand what to say and what things are better left unsaid.

Building relationships isn't just *how* we build a business. Relationships are also one of the reasons *why*. Birdie and I have seen our relationship strengthen and grow to levels that we never would've been able to enjoy if we were working jobs. One of the things that I think is a plus of the business we are involved in is the fact that we get to be together every day, all day. People ask us, "Don't you get tired of being with each other all the time?" I tell them, "We got married to be together all the time and that's what we like doing.

I have not built my business on material wealth; I have built it on relationships. The wealth is a result of the relationship serving and helping others be better. Birdie and I like to see people change their lives and know that we've been influential in helping many make changes. The only reason we are as successful as we are is because we've taught others how to dream and not only how to put in the effort required but to enjoy the journey. We've taught them how to love other people. It's a way of life we've been blessed with, and we want to bless others around the world. The secret of living is giving. It's dreaming. It's loving and caring for other people. Love and caring is the glue that holds a relationship together.

Become an encourager. Encouragement is something everybody needs all the time. Almost anyone who succeeds has developed the ability to give it. Look at some of life's great successes, I don't care what field it is. That guy got there because he was a big encourager. When you experience small successes you start believing in yourself. When you start believing in yourself, you start believing in other people. That's what encouragement is all about. Having the courage to go for what you want and building that same courage in other people.

When you find someone who is an encourager, get around them whenever you can. Who you decide to build relationships with determines the path your life will take, because the people you associate with will determine how you think, how you act, and where you'll end up. It's important to be aware of the attitudes of those people with whom you come in constant contact with. A person who is constantly critical, complaining, and is always pointing out others' faults will leave a negative impact on you. Negativity sells. It's everywhere. I always tell people not to pick up the newspaper or turn on the TV because there's so much negative. Negative is to help complainers who aren't going anywhere feel better about themselves. If these people were discussing success stories instead of negative, they'd have to accept that there are people out there who are doing something successful with their lives. They don't want to do that, because then their excuses wouldn't count anymore. They bring down others to put themselves up on a pedestal. Stay away from people with negative attitudes. Don't allow someone who has made the decision to fail disrupt your decision to succeed.

Seek out positive people. Seek out people who are achievers. Associating with positive people creates an atmosphere that promotes success. Make a point to be around them. Listen to their advice. Watch them as they relate to other individuals and learn from these encounters. I surround myself with ambitious, success-minded people. People with big dreams, who refuse to let failures get them down. As long as I can remember, it's been very important for me to be around these kinds of people because it helps me keep my own attitude at the highest altitude. Our attitudes empower each other. It's always been my dream to build a business and have friends like the friends I have now, and this dream has become reality which is very rewarding.

One of the most attractive things you can develop is an attitude of gratitude. It's important that you understand that. If you're grateful to people and you let them know you're grateful, they respond by going the extra mile for you the next time around. People like to be appreciated. They respond to those who are grateful with a desire to give them even more. They also respond to those who don't appear to be grateful with a desire to give them nothing at all. If you appreciate people and are grateful, you still have to learn how to show it skillfully. The art of saying, "thank you" is one that will open doors for you like magic. Look for opportunities to thank people. Look for as many opportunities as possible. Average people notice the obvious, but really successful people are always on the alert

> **People like to be appreciated. They respond to those who are grateful with a desire to give them even more.**

for what's not obvious in life. I've found that if you want to be really effective in developing relationships, you have to look for the things in people that no one else will catch. Watch for chances to show your appreciation for the little things that don't get mentioned. I always see the good in other people that they don't see in themselves. Then I help them believe it.

No matter what your profession is, success in life is about relationships. If you have good relationships, life is happy. If there's conflict or confusion between you and other people, life is hard. No amount of money can make you happy if you don't understand people and know how to get along with them. Try not to complicate things—just learn to be a friend and you'll discover what every successful person has already learned: it's not what you know, it's who you know, and it's not just who you know, it's the quality of the friendship with who you know.

A gossip is one who talks to you about others;
a bore is one who talks to you about himself;
and a brilliant conversationalist is one who talks to you about yourself.
**– Lisa Kirk**

People don't really care how much you know until they know how much you care.
**– Carett Robert**

There are two things people want more than sex and money...recognition and praise.
**– Dexter Yager**

Everyone has an invisible sign hanging around their neck
saying, "make me feel important."
**– Dale Carnegie**

No man becomes rich unless he enriches others.
**– Andrew Carnegie**

I can live for two months on one good compliment.
**– Mark Twain**

# Chapter 27

## Success is a system

Everyone has a system—it's either designed for success or for failure.
**- Dexter Yager**

This chapter is so important. I think that having a system for success is something all super-successful people have in common and everyone else should learn.

> **I create a system to create a predictable result.**

Wherever I have been successful in my life, behind that success is a system. I want to help others to achieve the same results, or better, than what I have achieved. I want them to achieve it faster and with less frustration and wasted energy. Everything I do, I do with an intended result in mind, and then I create a system to create an intended result. I've learned that the more time you have to take to think about the same things over and over, the more unproductive you are, so all my life I've been developing and perfecting systems to make me as productive as possible. My goal in doing this is to consistently achieve predictable results.

A system will make anything easier. Systems move you from a decision to an intended result in the most rapid possible way. I have a system for almost everything: for where I keep my car keys, for how I buy, wear, and pack my clothes, and for how I bring people into my business and teach them what they need to know. When I spend a day, as I do regularly, strategizing and teaching with an individual, couple, or group, I have a system for what I do and where I go. I stick with my system every single time—consistency is the key. My kids always know what to expect from me. They can predict what I would do in a given situation because I have always been consistent.

Anybody that has ever had any kind of success, and keeps it, has a system. A major part of that system is learning it. If you have a team, or you want to develop a team, having a system and following it consistently is critical for success, and will greatly duplicate and multiply your efforts.

To really make that system multiply, you have to keep it simple. I want to make it simple to follow, simple to teach, and then I reinforce the system with those on my team at every

**Systems may have little parts, but they swing big ideas.**

opportunity. If you don't have a system for success, you have a system for failure. If you have a hard time making decisions, you are making a decision to fail.

In W. Clement Stone's book, *The Success System That Never Fails*, every chapter has a picture of a door that says, "Little hinges swing big doors." It's not how little you are. It's how big the door is that you swing. Systems may have little parts but they swing big ideas.

The dictionary defines a system as "a regularly interacting or interdependent group of items forming a unified whole." For me, success is "the whole." A few years ago, before giving a talk to a large audience, I prayed God would help me to share the secrets of my success in the little time

> **If you don't have a system for success, you have a system for failure.**

I had, and this is what I came up with:

1. Learn what to do from the best. They know what they're talking about because they've performed it. Copy the best and take what you like from them. Copying is stealing, but learning something and then applying it is experience. When you've got experience, it's yours because you put your personality into it. It makes the difference.

2. Learn how to do something the best that you can. Not perfect, but the best you can.

3. Do it. Do it consistently. Practice it in front of anyone, anytime, as if your life depended upon winning them. Learn how to keep getting better. Only practice makes you better.

4. Find five to ten things you can't live without. That gives you the energy and the drive to succeed. You've got to have a reason. Money is not a reason. To say, "Well, if I was making $250,000 a year..." is not enough, because if you're not already making that much money, you can't relate to it. You've got to figure out what $250,000 a year could get you. Figure out that lifestyle and say, "I'm willing to have these things. It will take me 'x' amount of dollars a year to get them, so I'm going for them."

5. Go touch at least one of those dreams every day. I could have combined this with a previous step, but it is too important. Many people identify things they would like to have, but you double your odds of achieving them by associating with them regularly. It's like a courtship—I call it "courting your dream." You want a Cadillac or a Mercedes?

Go to the dealership every day. Most people will tell you, "I can't. I've got a job. I work 8:00 a.m. to 5:00 p.m. I get home, drive to a meeting, and I get back so late at night that the dealerships are closed." Great! That's when I go—when everything's closed. There's no traffic, and nobody's bothering you. I shop when everything's closed; it doesn't cost me a thing. I go once when it's open. Try it. It's sort of like having a picture of your girlfriend, but there's a huge difference between kissing the picture and kissing the girl. You've got to learn to draw the line on your goals. You've got to develop a system for setting goals and achieving them. Not until I do this, will I get this. It's not important whether or not I've got the money—I may have the cash right there in my pocket, but I set a goal to achieve something before I allow myself to have it. I will deprive myself until I have performed or achieved the goal. Then, when I get it, I know I deserve it because I set my goals and accomplished them. It's a system that works for me because it makes me perform. I set and draw my lines on *my* life, not the world. Go touch your dreams regularly, whatever they are, take the time to investigate and research them. You've got to have five to twenty goals that you are seeing daily, weekly, and monthly.

> **Give yourself time to learn a successful system and then to implement it.**

6. Every time somebody rejects you, your plan, or your dreams, visualize yourself being in a superior position to them in the future. Success is the best revenge.

7. Treat those who laugh at you with respect and love. Why? You've already decided that you're better than they are and you're going to go prove it. You've got a superior brain. Are you going to use your body to show that your brain is superior?

> It's not important whether or not I've got the money—I may have the cash right there in my pocket, but I set a goal to achieve something before I allow myself to have it.

8. Out-dream, out-work, and out-love everyone. I'm going to love them when nobody can understand why I love them. Out-working them without the love, without the dream, and without the giving isn't enough. You've got to pull it all together.

9. Out-pray everyone. No excuses. Everything depends on God and my faith in Him, which is proven by my works.

10. I'm going to give God all the credit because He's done it all.

A great pleasure in life is doing what people say you cannot do. Winners learn to live on that. When people tell me that I can't do something, I'm thinking, "Who died and made you king? How do you know more about me than I know about me?" When I let someone tell me that, I'm letting them make the decision. Either way, winning or losing is our decision. The secret of happiness is not in doing what one likes, but in liking what one does. So many people come to Birdie and I and say, "This business is not my cup of tea; it's not my bag." The truth of the matter is they haven't decided what they wanted enough to understand that this is a thing that can get them what they want. Along the line, they've got to find out what they're willing to do and learn what they enjoy about doing it.

Here's a success system that works: First, know that success is a decision. After you make the decision, a vision will follow. It has to become a commitment and then a habit before it becomes a way of life. It'll be a constant struggle. When you're struggling, It's easy for you to say, "Well, this must not be for me. I ought to quit." Give yourself time to learn a successful system and then to implement it. A struggle is where you get your knowledge. The struggle is where you get tough. Then success comes, and everybody tells everybody else (including you) how lucky you are! They don't understand the journey. They don't know how important a system is. Everybody thinks that success is supposed to be easy.

Working hard is critical, but the definition of "working smart" is using a system for success. A system compliments my efforts, supplements my efforts, and multiplies my efforts, but if I don't put forth my best effort, there's nothing to compliment, supplement, or multiply.

Discretion is the enemy of duplication
- **Ray Kroc**

# Chapter 28

## Success is all about serving

*Leadership is a serving relationship with the intent of helping someone become better, more responsible, and self-reliant.*
**– Dexter Yager**

Martin Luther King, Jr. said, "Everybody can be great... because anybody can serve." Live a life that leaves everyone better than you found them.

Proverbs 11:24, 25 of the Living Bible says, "It is possible to give away and become richer! It is also possible to hold on too tightly and lose everything. Yes, the liberal man shall be rich! By watering others, he waters himself." You were created to change and help someone else.

If you want to be somebody, take a person that thinks they're nobody and treat them like a somebody. When you treat everybody like they're somebody they'll think you're somebody, not because you're so great, but because you make them feel great. I believe in you. I see in you more than you see in you.

Invest in the success of others. When you help someone up a mountain, you'll find yourself close to the summit, too. If you want others to improve, let them hear the nice things you say about them. People will treat you the way you view them. Find the good in everyone. Draw out their strengths not their weaknesses. You'll find that one of the best ways to lead people is to make them feel you are behind them. Most people can live for two months on five words of praise and a pat on the back.

A good coach is building a team. He doesn't get jealous of his best player and he doesn't neglect his ordinary players. He's trying to put together a whole team of "best players." He teaches them to be team players. Doesn't make any difference who the star is, he wants the team to win the game. To be the minor player on the winning team is better than being the best player on the losing team. See, a coach can always see more in the athlete than what the athlete sees. That's why he's willing to coach them.

When reaching out to help others, don't give till it hurts—give until it feels good. "No man was ever honored for what he received. Honor has been the reward for what he gave" (Calvin Coolidge).

As you build your business, understand you invest your life and time into people. At first, those who won't listen, we will still try to teach. But if we keep investing time and money in people who won't listen, then we need to move on. They've got to be hungry enough to learn. Not everybody's going to succeed because not everybody listens.

**We have our success story because we've helped more people go farther than anybody else in this industry ever has. It's just that simple.**

I believe that one of the marks of true greatness is to develop greatness in others. "There are three keys to more abundant living: caring about others, daring for others and sharing with others" (William Ward). I have never made money on anything before my people were making money on it. Normally they were making money on it before I was.

I have found that really great men have the unique perspective that greatness is not deposited in them to stay but rather to flow through them into others. "We make a living by what we get, but we make a life by what we give" (Norman MacEwan). Assign yourself the purpose of making others happy and successful. There are two types of people in the world: those who come into a room and say, "Here I am!" and those who come in and say, "Ah, there you are!"

When you give out of love and concern then you help others. But sometimes more importantly, you learn to help yourself. The way to get up is to help somebody else get up. The way to learn, many times, is to teach somebody else. You have got to be willing to give. You've got to care, to be cared for. You've got to be willing to share, for somebody to share with you.

Everybody counts. People have problems every place you go. They need love. They need caring. People say, "How have you impacted so many people? How do you care about people?" We get involved in their life. Everybody is important. And if we want to be important we've got to make everybody else feel important. Because what you give is what you get. We've got to be willing to step out in life if we want the good things to happen. We've got to be willing to put our image at risk. Otherwise, we're not going to make a difference. So as we listen to people, they'll listen to us. It's simple whether its business, whether it's the Lord; it makes a difference.

Help others step up. Success comes from helping others. We have our success story because we've helped more people go farther than anybody else in this industry ever has.

It's just that simple. We had to find them. We had to go through a lot of people to find a few that have done a lot. You can too.

We can all experience success, but how much success do you want? How much do you want to help others discover?

Think of me smaller than you because you can become bigger than me. Anybody can become bigger than me but you'll have your tongue hanging out when you go by. What's this line between us? It's a line of communication. It's my hand reaching down to help you succeed. I want you to succeed but you've got to want it more for you than I want it for you. It's your business. If you're not willing to do the work, I cannot do it for you, but I can teach you. And I'm going to help you

**Help others step up. Success comes from helping others.**

and if some of your friends want some help, we'll go work it and we'll look and see the one that wants it the worst and will work it the hardest. I remember back when I sold cars my sales manager told me, "Dexter, one thing you've got to learn to do is say 'no'." And that's always been the hardest thing in my life is to say 'no' to somebody. Sometimes the best thing you can do for others is to say, "No."

I remember my first stroke. A month in the hospital. Eight neurologists said I'd never get out of the wheelchair. I'd never walk again. Okay? That was their decision, not mine. I felt that I was happy to get out of the hospital, happy to be alive. But I'd been beaten up enough verbally in the hospital. I came home and offered Birdie a divorce. I said, "You don't need to live with this crippled mess. It's not your fault. You're a gorgeous 46 year-old girl; you don't need this kind of baggage." The next day I got up and there was a card next to the bed. She'd written across it, "The only thing that counts is we have each other." You know, it's only a little statement. It's only a little phrase, but it meant my world at that time. Husbands and wives, on your way to help others don't forget to help "each other." People need to be praised and loved. We're criticized and condemned enough in the outside world.

One of my success secrets is to fall in love with somebody

> **One of my success secrets is to fall in love with somebody else I can serve.**

else I can serve. Growth comes from somebody who loves you more than you love yourself, sees more in you than you see in yourself, but knows you must be mentored, knows that you must bring the problems to them for them to help you solve. We don't solve other people's problems. We don't tell people what to do. We sit down and help them decide what to do, unless they're going in the wrong direction. When they're going in the wrong direction, we simply tell them, "This is the wrong direction. Get in the right direction."

Do your best to never give up on a person. It takes faith. You never stop loving a person. That's love. It doesn't matter if they go off here and they do this and they do that, and they bungle up this and they bungle up that. You don't have to stop loving them. You've got to get the love down pat. You've got to understand what love is. Love is a decision. You either decide to love somebody, or you decide not to love somebody. And once you have decided to love them, then it's easy to love them. But it's not always easy to respect them. A person earns your respect. They don't earn your love. And you've got to learn how to separate the two in your mind. In certain circumstances it's our job to get out there and say, "You can make it!"

Hope is something that we can give to each other. Hope is something friends give to each other. Hope is something we've got to keep giving. The more we give it, the more we get. Spread the hope around.

A rising tide raises all ships.
**– Anonymous**

He sat down and summoned the twelve.
"So you want first place? Then take the last place. Be the servant of all."
**– Mark 9:35 (The Message)**

Outstanding leaders go out of their way to boost the self-esteem of their personnel. If people believe in themselves,
it's amazing what they can accomplish.
**– Sam Walton**

Give a man a fish, and he'll eat for a day.
Teach him how to fish and he'll eat forever.
**- Chinese Proverb**

It is one of the beautiful compensations of this life
that no one can sincerely try to help another without helping himself.
**– Charles Dudley**

Service is the rent we pay for being on this earth.
**– Marian Wright Edelman**

# Chapter 29

## Success is staying mentally broke

Ah, but a man's reach must exceed his grasp, or what's a heaven for?
**- Robert Browning**

One of the most important success habits is to learn to have your dream grow as you grow. I remember back at an early point in our business, I had certain dreams and goals, and I went after them. After I accomplished them, I didn't know where to go because I didn't know how to grow. Since then, I learned how to develop dreams, and I learned how to keep myself mentally broke. You'll find that every super wealthy person in the world has to learn how to keep themselves mentally broke. Most people are trying to find security and that's death. When you find security, you find your little hole, you sit in there, and you hide. You've got to leave space in your mind to grow, to do better.

> Most people are trying to find security and that's death.

The more successful you become the greater the temptation is to coast. But really, success creates more opportunities. To see them we must stay hungry in our minds. I've seen people that reached high levels in life which were a good blast-off point for the future, but it was a dying point for them.

Your most valuable asset is the gold mine that's between

your own two ears, but a gold mine is only valuable when you work it. You've got to work your claim. You can have a claim up in the mountains, and nobody knows about it but you and you live poor and you die poor.

You've got to think bigger. We set our needs. We set our energy level, our dream level. If we cannot dream it, we cannot get it.

You've got to keep yourself uncomfortable. As soon as people get comfortable in life, they start slowing down. They start taking days off or nights off. They start relaxing more, and they start performing less. You've got to keep the burn.

When you want something badly enough you'll change, and you won't move forward

---

**...a gold mine is only valuable when you work it.**

---

until you change. When I had a stroke I had bad eating habits. I remember confessing stupidity. "If I cannot have what I want to eat, then life's not worth living." I had to come to a point in life where I decided, "Change that pattern." I put this whole ugly picture together one night. If I didn't eat right, I was going to die young. After Birdie buried me, she'd be lonely, and she'd fall in love with some other guy. So the guy she would probably pick would be a guy that was the opposite of me. He wouldn't be a tightwad. He'd be willing to spend my wad. He'd be willing to entertain her. He wouldn't pay the disciplines I pay. He would try to reach her from another side. He'd love driving my cars and sleeping in my bed with my wife. When you look at the worst side, you'll change. We can tell you how but you've got to make the decision, and you've got to understand the difference between real gold and fool's gold.

Somebody asked Henry Ford years ago, "Henry don't you have enough money?"

He said, "No, I need just a little bit more."

That's the way you and I've got to live our life. We need just a little bit more for tomorrow and a little bit more for today.

You know there's a great man, John Ruskin, who wrote a saying, "If I rest, I rust."

> **By being mentally "broke" you can become physically rich.**

I used to hang that on my wall back when I was 25 years old. I hung that on my wall to haunt me so I wouldn't rest because I want to have a drive and to get something accomplished.

Somebody says, "Yeah, but how do you handle the guy that's more successful than you?" Well nine times out of ten, you'll find him saying, "I've got all I want." Number one, that's a lie. If it isn't, then he's sick. If he had all he wanted, why is he going to work tomorrow? It's like the same guy that lies to you and says, "Money doesn't mean anything to me." Fine, give me all you've got.

Feed your mind the opportunity that is in front of you, not just what you've already accomplished. Only hungry minds can grow.

When we keep our minds "empty" for opportunity, we don't let satisfaction become a hindrance to future growth. Being mentally broke creates the space that ideas and dreams can fill. By being mentally "broke" you can become physically rich.

# Chapter 29

Lord grant that I may always desire more than I can accomplish.

**- Anonymous**

# Chapter 30

## Success allows no excuses!

Some people make money, some make excuses. But no one makes both.
**- Dexter Yager**

I had to laugh at it. Here was a guy who had his foot operated on the week before, and he was spending all his energy and passion trying to get some signed excuses so he would not have to go to work. It's amazing; winners take everything in stride. Losers try to make anything as an excuse to get out of stride. Do you understand the difference? There's job mentality and there's success mentality. And so many people have job mentality. They want to know how many sick days they have so they can plan to get sick. They want to get them. Winners don't have time to get sick.

The worst buy is an alibi. Every one of us that has gone forward has struggled. I know the stories; we lived it. But no excuse is acceptable for my failure. All the doctors' excuses when I'd come out of the hospital were not acceptable. My Lord is stronger. My faith is stronger. There are no excuses. Winners do it in spite of anything.

When you're good at making excuses, it's hard to excel at anything else. The book of Proverbs says, "Work brings profit; talk brings poverty." Don't make excuses; make progress.

Excuses are the nails used to build a house of failure. An alibi is egotism wrong side out. "Ninety-nine percent of the failures come from people who have the habit of making excuses" (George Washington Carver). A man can fail many times, but he isn't a failure until he begins to blame somebody or something else.

We could've found excuses that other people find, but winners don't accept cheap excuses because you don't find them on the road to success. It's overcoming the junk that makes you tough and better.

Everybody who quits has their list of why they quit. I just want to warn you that when you step out on your own you'll experience a miracle in your life, and you're going to have warfare. You're going to have a battle surrounding your dream and you're going to have to fight. And it's your choice how you fight it and whether you fight it. But we chose, a long time ago, to fight it with all our might and with God's help.

> The man who really wants to do something finds a way; the other man finds an excuse.

A few years ago, a friend of mine was in Korea, and he jumped on a land mine. He came out a mess. Face all scarred up. Eyes blown out. They sewed fake eyes in. They were always open. His fingers were blown off. One hundred percent disabled. Blind. He used to stand up and say there are some people with 20/20 vision who cannot see anything. Even though he is blind, he can see opportunity better than almost anyone I know.

Never let a challenge become an alibi. Quitting and failures always begin with alibis, justification, pity trips and feeling sorry for yourself. "The bread of deceit is sweet to a man; but afterwards his mouth shall be filled with gravel," (Proverbs 20:17).

The man who really wants to do something finds a way; the other man finds an excuse. I used to accept everybody's excuses. I understand the struggle. I understand they give you excuses. I no longer accept excuses from anybody. I am not going to be their prescription for failure. If that's their choice, that's their choice. Success is a matter of luck; just ask any failure.

We have to learn to accept responsibility for things in our life. You're either responsible or you're irresponsible—there's no in between. We need to have a positive outlook, but that doesn't mean we avoid reality. Everyone faces challenges and problems. Success lies in dealing with them. If you want to be successful, there's no one to blame but yourself, because until someone takes the blame, nothing will change. And if nothing changes, nothing will change. You'll keep getting the results you've always been getting. Until the pain of change is less than the pain of staying the same, nothing will change.

Something I heard coach Lou Holtz say is, "The biggest thing that's changed in our society over the last 50 years is that back then, people thought more about their responsibilities and obligations. Today people think about their rights and privileges."

Back when I was overeating, one of the things I never ate was asparagus. Only recently have I begun to eat it. There's about a half a dozen things on my former diet I wouldn't touch, but I eat now because they're good for me.

I had to learn to create the taste. People say, "are you really like that?" I don't have a choice; I'm going to like it. I'm going to learn to like it. That's what success is. So many people go, "Well there's no way, when we were starting to build our business, no way that you'd get me to do what you're doing. There's no way that we'd work that hard. There's no way we'd do that. There's no way." Well then...there's no way you'll succeed!

I'm going to challenge you to get rid of your objections, to throw out your excuses, to do something that you've never done before, to commit yourself to thirty days of being tired, thirty days of rejection, thirty days of being proud of yourself. I'm going to challenge you to thirty days of daring to dream. Daring to reach out and have your hand slapped, daring to stick your chin out and let somebody hit it, daring to step into a ring where you risk defeat. You'll see then. You'll take the first step. The magic will have started for you and alibis and excuses will be afraid to hand around you.

Any guy who has ever walked the tightrope understands he must stay focused from where he's at and always look where he's going. A tightrope walker does not look at the rope, he looks at the goal. He feels the rope with his feet. If he looks down, he's going down. He has to look for his goal. And you can't look at the crap in life. You got to look at the dream, the goal.

The best is yet to come. Don't be stupid enough to walk out and find something wrong with anything. Whatever was wrong, it was for somebody else, not for you. It wasn't your blessing, so don't take it as your curse. Count the blessing; count the best.

I remember my friend Jim was excited and he was showing me a little bit around the town. He showed me his house and his cabin that he gets away to. I'm watching the vehicles on one side, he's watching trees on the other, and he backs smack into a tree. I said, "Jim, you smashed the back window out." He laughed, and you know, there wasn't anything you could do. "Yeah," he said, "Now I guess I probably smashed up the back end." We didn't even get out and look. The tree wasn't moving. You couldn't change anything about it. But you know it costs just as much to fix it whether you're rich or you're broke. It doesn't make any difference.

Most people will tell you successful people are materialistic, but really, broke people are materialistic. A broke guy would have gotten out of that vehicle, sat there, bawled for an hour and cried the blues for the next two weeks. Everybody he ran into would hear about his terrible fate. Bad things happen to me, just like everyone else. See, a winner does what has to be done. A winner wins. And it's his choice.

**Excuses are something you hide behind so that you don't succeed.**

You have got to see the bright side of everything in life. A winner will see the bright side, and a loser will see the dark clouds always coming in through life. What are you seeing today? Are you seeing the bright side of life? Or are you seeing the dark clouds that drift in?

I believe that you can find any person and an excuse for them to fail, but I'm not looking for excuses. I'm looking for reasons to win. I'm looking for people who want to win.

You know today really is the first day of the rest of your excuse-free life. You can be anything you want to be, anything. Don't give me your excuses. I don't want to hear excuses. Excuses are something you hide behind so that you don't succeed.

If you're really going to succeed then excuses are useless.
**- Dexter Yager**

# Chapter 31

## Eternal Success

Success, real success, is a relationship with the Lord that's constantly growing
**- Dexter Yager**

We all want to experience success in our lives, but we must realize we are only going to be here on this earth for a short time. We are going to be dead (physically) a lot longer than we will be alive. Where do you plan on spending eternity? Have you thought about it?

In this life's pursuit, you're not alone. My faith is the most important part of my life. I thought about whether or not I should add this chaptert, but I realized that if I don't share my faith, then I've left out the most important part of my success. I remember praying to God that if He would help me in my business and become my partner, then I would give Him all the credit. So, I realized I didn't really have a choice on whether or not I should include it.

The Lord is with you too, if you ask Him. If you've got a dream and a passion for that dream, then you can be anything that you and God work together to design. I believe we should follow Mary Lyon's advice: "Trust in God and do something."

The most profound truth is "Jesus loves me." The most profound revelation is "This I know." Don't put a question mark where God puts a period.  Why is it that so many church members who say "Our Father" on Sunday go around the rest of the week acting like orphans?

Most people's lives have been spared by God so many times and all they can think about is, "What a crappy life I have. I don't get any good breaks." They've quit thanking God for the miracles He created. They don't appreciate it. If you cannot count your blessings every day, then you've gone the wrong way.

"If a man stands with his right foot on a hot stove and his left foot in a freezer, some statisticians would assert that, on the average, he is comfortable" (Oral Hygiene). Nothing could be further from the truth. God doesn't want us to live our lives with one foot in heaven and one foot in the world. He wants all of us.

**When God is number one, everything else adds up.**

D.L. Moody said, "It does not take long to tell where a man's treasure is. In fifteen minutes of conversation with most men, you can tell whether their treasures are on earth or in heaven." As a young man, Billy Graham prayed, "God, let me do something—anything—for you." Look at the result of that simple but heartfelt prayer.

When God is number one, everything else adds up.

Tommy Barnett reflected, "The deeper I dig the deeper He digs." To increase value, get to know God. Pray to the Father, "I want to be in your will, not in your way."

Oswald Chambers advises us: "Get into the habit of dealing with God about everything. Unless in the first waking moment of the day you learn to fling the door wide back and let God in, you will work on a wrong level all day; but swing the door wide open and pray to your Father in secret, and every public thing will be stamped with the presence of God." Stop every day and look at the size of God.

God gives to those who give the most. You cannot out give God, whether it's money, love, care, vision, or faith. Success is long-term proof of faith extended.

The man who puts God first will find God with him right up to the end. "In everything you do, put God first, and He will direct you and crown your efforts with success" (Prov. 3:6, LB).

> **God gives to those who give the most.**

The fact is that anyone who doesn't believe in miracles is not a realist. Look around, nothing is more real than miracles. When you leave God out, you'll find yourself without any invisible means of support. Nothing great has ever been achieved except by those who dared to believe that God inside them was superior to circumstance.

How do I deepen my faith? Pray, but that's not the only way. A lot of people only pray, and that's why they don't get anything. God's waiting for them to get up and do something after they pray, and they don't.

Here's another way to deepen your faith. It's got to be a daily thing. You've got to be seeking more faith and more wisdom every day. It's not just faith that you need. It's wisdom. So many people come up and say to me, "How do you have so much wisdom?" I keep asking for it. I'm always asking for it, and act with faith that God will grant it.

If the preacher isn't preaching positively, get yourself out of there. You're not there to keep a seat warm. You're not there to satisfy men or your neighbors. You're there for you. If you aren't getting fed, and if you aren't getting uplifted by the word of God, then get out.

Author Ken Blanchard said that the best partnership you can possibly make in business is a partnership with God. When you bring God in as your partner you do three things. You bring in God who conceived of the plan. You bring in Christ who modeled the plan. You bring in the Holy Spirit as the daily operating officer. According to Ken Blanchard, it's just the best deal. There's no better merger you can make than a merger with God. When God is part of your life as the chief operating officer, you truly do become the master of your own destiny.

Constantly, we've had people pull things, play games, do power plays. You name it; people do that. That's life. Ultimately you've got to know God's in control. If God is all you have, then He is all you need.

Success from us is what God wants to see. It is up to you and me. So, for you I must ask, what's it going to be? I built my business with the attitude that it all counts on me, I pray like it all counts on Him, and I work like everybody's going to quit.

I have a very best friend in my life. This person and his son are the two closest friends I've ever had. No matter what I've done, they've always loved me, they've always forgiven me, and they've seen the best of me. That one major friend is the most materialistic person in the whole world. He's materialistic because He owns everything. He created everything. He is my mentor and my leader. His name is God.

"God never made a promise that was too good to be true" (D. L. Moody). When you join together with Him in His plan, things that were impossible now become possible.

The things which are impossible with men are possible with God.
**– Luke 18:27**

Alive, I'm Christ's messenger; dead, I'm his bounty.
Life versus even more life! I can't lose.
**– Phillipians 1:21**

# PRODUCTION

"I do not believe a man can ever leave his business. He ought to think of it by day and dream of it by night. It is nice to plan to do one's work in office hours, to take up the work in the morning. It is perfectly possible to do that if one is so constituted as to be willing through all of his life to accept direction, to be an employee, possibly a responsible employee, but not a director or manager of anything. A manual laborer must have a limit on his hours; otherwise, he will wear himself out. If he intends to remain always a manual laborer, then he should forget about his work when the whistle blows, but if he intends to go forward and do anything, the whistle is only a signal to start thinking over the day's work in order to discover how it might be done better.

The man who has the largest capacity for work and thought is the man who is bound to succeed. I cannot pretend to say, because I do not know, whether the man who works always, who never leaves his business, who is absolutely intent upon getting ahead, and who, therefore does get ahead, is happier than the man who keeps his office hours for both his brain and his hands. It is not necessary for anyone to decide the question. A ten horsepower engine will not pull as much as twenty. The man who keeps his brain office hours limits his horsepower. If he is satisfied to pull only the load that he has, well and good, that is his affair—but he must not complain if another who has increased his horsepower pulls more than he does.

Leisure and work bring different results. If a man wants leisure and gets it, then he has no cause to complain. But he cannot have both leisure and the results of work."

**– Henry Ford**

## Other books by Dexter Yager

Don't Let Anybody Steal Your Dream

Dynamic People Skills

Everything I Know At The Top, I Learned At The Bottom

Millionaire Mentality

Ordinary Men, Extraordinary Heroes


## Other books by John L. Mason

An Enemy Called Average

Ask...Life's Most Important Answers
Are Found In Asking The Right Questions

Conquering An Enemy Called Average

Know Your Limits – Then Ignore Them

Let Go Of Whatever Makes You Stop

The Impossible Is Possible

You're Born An Original – Don't Die A Copy